Great Headlines Ir

How To Write Attention-Grabbing He.
More Prospects... More Customers... an(
-- Version 2.1 --

Published by:
Success Track Communications
Pickering, Ontario Canada
ISBN: 978-0-9811807-2-4

Author Contact:
Robert Boduch
rboduch@rogers.com
http://bizprofitbuilder.com

Cover photo credit: *Grafixar - Indianapolis, Indiana*

TABLE OF CONTENTS

GREAT HEADLINES INSTANTLY
Version 2.1

How To Write Powerful, Attention-Grabbing Headlines That
Pull In More Prospects, More Customers And More Profits,
NOW!

Introduction

There is no more valuable skill you could acquire as a marketer, than the skill of creating attention-grabbing headlines. It's a skill that once mastered, can be used anytime, anywhere, to attract more prospects, increase your sales, improve your cash flow, and boost your profits.

Headlines are your "front line" to any market. It's the first thing most prospects see. Your headline is your one big chance to interest and influence a selected audience with your message.

If you want your messages to get noticed… if you want to be heard… if you want to make a splash in the marketplace… you need to have headlines that not only work -- but work extremely well.

Nothing is more important to the success of every communication you ever produce than the headlines that act as "opening statements". Headlines play a crucial role. However, most marketers and business owners fail to recognize the monumental impact a single headline can have on their overall results.

As your introductory point of contact, headlines are often your *only* chance to capture the attention and stimulate the interest of the people you must reach to achieve the results you want. Headlines are often referred to as an "ad for an ad". They set the stage for the audience and they either grab a prospect's attention, or they don't. This rings true whether the document is a lengthy sales letter, a tiny classified ad, or a complete book. Headlines reign supreme.

Great headlines create excitement, anticipation, and enthusiasm for more. A single headline has the power to launch a multi-million dollar business... or to turn a losing campaign into a highly-successful one.

When your headline succeeds, you've overcome the greatest obstacle facing all marketers; you've won over -- at least for the time being -- a receptive audience for your message.

If, on the other hand, your headline fails to attract and interest an audience, not only will your promotion falter, but the remainder of your ad, brochure, web site, or article, will be rendered completely useless. Any body copy quickly becomes irrelevant when the headline fails to capture interested readers.

With the information you hold in your hands, you have everything you need to craft an unlimited number of arresting, provocative, compelling, and...*money-making* headlines.

This manual is actually a "blueprint" for creating successful headlines -- quickly and easily. It's your complete guide to writing winning headlines for virtually any application or purpose.

The information presented here applies to everything from classified ads and sales letters, to newsletter articles and web pages. I've tried to deliver the most important, profit-producing information available about creating riveting, attention-grabbing headlines that pull prospects in with the unstoppable force of a powerful magnet. And I'm confident that if you apply these concepts, you will improve your results.

When you've acquired the skill of writing winning headlines, you'll possess the capability of crafting compelling ads and marketing materials of all kinds. Headline writing is the essence of good copy writing. It's all about generating concise, power-packed statements that ignite interest and desire. Isn't that the "heart and soul" of the best sales letters and direct marketing packages?

Headlines... subheads... bullet points... postscripts... all of these components are in effect -- headlines. So you're not just learning headline writing, you're gaining valuable skills that can transform your marketing efforts for a lifetime. It's impossible to put a price tag on the kind of value you'll get by applying, testing and tweaking this information to suit.

Do these ideas actually work?

Yes… absolutely!

I've been writing headlines as part of my work for clients over the past several years. I've also used these techniques and formulas to create headlines for my own projects. I can promise you this with absolute conviction: these ideas will make your promotional efforts better than they were before and probably a whole lot better than the competition.

But you don't have to take my word for it. Many of the exciting and profitable ideas you'll discover here, have been used by a number of marketing experts with diverse, yet very successful backgrounds. You'll find interviews with three such experts in Appendix A of this book.

Often the difference between a winning headline and one that fails may boil down to just a word or two. But the results can be so radically different, that you may have trouble believing them for yourself. However, believe them you will when you witness this for yourself.

Testing is the only way to inexpensively prove the effectiveness of your headline. It's always a good idea to test response on a small scale before making the commitment to invest a substantial amount on your advertising.

One marketer discovered the value of testing by trying 4 different headlines for a diet product, over a 3-month period. The sales material remained identical. Only the headline was different in each case.

The headlines were as follows:

1. *"Breakthrough New Diet Product!"*
2. *"A New Diet Revolution!"*
3. *"How A "Texas Housewife" Lost 23.5 Pounds In 32 Days!"*
4. *"Dieting Secrets Of A Desperate Housewife!"*

Every individual response was carefully tracked and recorded. The actual documented results may surprise you.

Total sales were 165 units over this testing period.

Here's a breakdown of the results each specific headline produced:

1. 13 Sales (8% of total sales)
2. 8 Sales (5% of total sales)
3. 98 Sales (59% of total sales)
4. 46 Sales (28% of total sales)

As you can see, **the most successful headline produced nearly 12 times the number of sales of the least responsive headline.** That's a huge variation. What a discovery to make early on in the marketing process! This is the kind of information that can help you make a fortune as a marketer. The key in this case, was the headline and the ability to determine the most effective appeal to use. That's the value of testing. Use it and it can help you find a winner too.

All of the ideas you'll discover here can be applied to any kind of communication. They work in good times and bad -- when the economy is thriving as well those periods when conditions aren't so favorable.

Most of the ideas presented here are based on human nature and the emotional stimulus that captures attention and generates interest. While the actual words change over time, many of the same appeals that worked years ago, still work today. You see, human behavior hasn't changed much over the years. We react to the same emotional triggers our forefathers did. So, using these strong emotional appeals is one of the secrets to making headlines work for you.

This product is a collection of strategies and techniques accumulated over the years. Some ideas have come from recognized experts through their books, seminars, articles, and interviews. Other ideas, have been developed through practice. Every key piece of information I've ever discovered about creating great headlines has been included here for your benefit.

You can tuck this book away on a shelf somewhere and forget about it -- or you can use it to start writing headlines that increase your response rates and consequently, your bank account. The choice is yours.

The world is waiting for your message. Will they hear it? Well, that's entirely up to you.

This project was originally launched with the intent of sharing this information exclusively with other entrepreneurs and business owners. But as it developed, I realized just how many different groups of people could benefit from this material. Copywriters, webmasters, newsletter publishers (both online and print), magazine writers, self-publishers, advertisers, marketing managers, salespeople -- the list of people who could benefit from this goes on and on. Many people of various avenues and backgrounds could profit from the wealth of tips, techniques, formulas, and examples presented on these pages. I hope you find the same kind of value yourself.

If you're a business owner, the success of every promotional piece you ever use hinges on your headline. For a marketing manager, your future employment rides on the success of a single campaign. The right headline can make all the difference. For a writer, the ability to grab attention and interest is crucial – and this is where the headlines you choose come into play.

So wherever you are and however you choose to use these ideas, I guarantee you this: your headlines will be much more effective if you use this information wisely. More prospects will notice your message and be made aware of your product and the benefits it affords. This can only mean more interested, highly-qualified prospects… more eager customers… and more dollars in your pocket.

If you carefully absorb this material, study the examples, and try only a few of the suggested formulas… I'm certain you'll be delighted with your new results and your investment in this book will be easily justified.

Are you ready to get started?

I have just 4 simple requests before we begin:

1. **Read every page.** You can go ahead and skim through it first if you wish. But if you want to get the most from this work, please take the time to read and comprehend each page. I've tried to explain these ideas in a way that could be easily understood and assimilated.

2. **Keep this reference handy.** There's nothing like having the right tool in your greatest time of need. Whenever you need to produce any kind of written communication, you'll need to create headlines. At times you'll be rushed. But you now have hundreds of samples that can be adopted for your own purposes -- whenever time is in short supply, making any writing task that much easier.

3. **Be willing to try new things.** Keep an open mind. You never know what idea -- however unsuitable it might at first appear -- can develop into a hugely successful headline that literally opens the floodgates to a non-stop river of response. I encourage you to *push the envelope* and try new things. But only after you've gained a solid grasp of the basics first.

4. **Don't attempt to use all of these ideas at once.** Keep it simple. Be selective and apply those tips, techniques, strategies and templates that resonate and seem most appropriate for your product, market, and objectives. *Use whatever works to get where you want to go.* Some ideas are contradictory in nature -- but equally potent. All can be used with ample effectiveness in given the right situation.

This product was produced to help you create your own compelling headlines on demand. Any single idea or example could be the catalyst that triggers your next big winner.

By applying the various tips, techniques, and processes, you'll find your mind opening up to even bigger and better ideas.

Don't limit yourself. Listen to your ideas and be willing to test any that appear to have even a remote chance of success. That's how truly breakthrough headlines evolve.

One headline can literally change your life. And now… you have the tools and the background material to write superb headlines anytime you want, as often you wish. I hope you use this resource to create headlines of your own that produce outstanding results for you. And when they do, I'd love to hear about it.

Finally, this manual is written in a simple, straightforward manner. It's a conversation between you and me. For simplicity, I've used the masculine pronoun on occasion, throughout this work. This was done merely to avoid the incessant use of "him or her" when referring to a third-party subject. No offense is intended... hopefully, none is taken. It is nothing more than a grammatical convention used for convenience. I encourage you to focus on the information instead, for that's where the true value is. Now... use it for all it's worth.

11 Specific Skills You'll Acquire From Reading This Book

1. How To Write A Winning Headline For Any Product, Service, or Application

2. How To Improve Any Existing Headline

3. Effective Word Selection For Maximum Impact

4. How To Edit A Headline And Refine It To Its Most Concise Form

5. How To Recognize A Winner From A Loser

6. How To Make Any Form Of Written Communication Much More Powerful

7. How To Extend The Capabilities Of A Headline With Additional Firepower

8. The Essence Of Effective Copy Writing

9. Idea Generation Techniques For More Powerful Headline Content

How To Get The Attention Of Your Target Prospects

10. How To Make Your Headline Stand Out Anywhere With Visual Enhancements

Chapter 1

The Purpose of Headlines and Why Creating a Powerful, Irresistible Headline Is The Most Valuable Thing You Can Do

What Is A Headline Anyway?

How would you define the headline?

In the simplest of terms, a headline might be described as the 'lead-in" or "opening" in any type of communication. An effective headline consists of a carefully selected group of words that does any, or all of the following:

- *Communicate a benefit*
- *Introduce a compelling offer*
- *Reveal news*

Regardless of the approach, every successful headline is directed at a specific audience. The intention is to:

1) Attract the attention of the largest possible target audience and...
2) Arouse their interest and ignite their desire for more.

As the lead-in, your headline plays a major role. It's the headline that must do the selling job on the entire ad, article, brochure, web site -- or any other application you happen to be working on.

Your headline either grabs attention from the start, or it doesn't. If it fails to attract a sufficient readership, nothing else matters much as far as your promotion goes. A headline that fails, dooms the entire effort.

Ideally, you want to make your reader or prospect "rubberneck" to pay attention to your message, the same way you would pay attention to a fire truck or police cruiser on the side of the road. Use whatever tools and techniques you have available to interrupt the mental focus of passers-by so they give all your words their undivided attention. That's what a good headline can do for you; *capture attention and fuel interest.*

What Is It About Headlines That Make Them So Important?

Headlines are (or should be) the first thing someone sees the moment your message appears before them. Headlines provide you with your best chance to pull prospects inside to the heart of your message. Any communication that lacks an effective and direct headline or opening, can only attract a small fraction of its full potential audience.

If the headline seems interesting to the reader, chances are, they'll continue reading. And that's exactly what you want them to do. For you to achieve the desired results, your prospects must read beyond the headline and take some kind of action, as detailed in the body copy of your message.

In all forms of communication, "selling" is what it's all about. It may be a product, a service, an idea, or a concept -- whatever it is, you're trying to interest and persuade prospects to accept your proposition. The mission is always to influence the audience. You want the other person to walk a road of agreement with you -- to "buy" into your ideas.

Headlines are vital to gaining *agreement.* The headline has to *sell* the reader on the rest of the message. If the headline is appealing, the reader is inclined to continue on. If it fails to attract interest, the reader's gone in a flash, never to return. The result: you lose your audience and any possible chance at gaining a new prospect or making a sale.

It's crucial that your headline draws an audience to your message. You've got to burst out of the gate with your strongest, most provocative, explosive handful of words... something that compels your best prospects to read further and to take action to gain the full, promised benefit.

Headlines can make or break any advertisement, marketing communication, or campaign. A poorly-conceived headline can completely neutralize even the finest written body copy from the best-paid writer in the world. Body copy -- and that includes everything beyond the headline -- doesn't get a fair reading when the headline fails to attract attention in the first place.

11

So it makes sense to focus your greatest efforts on evolving a headline that is attention-getting, interest-inspiring, and the most compelling collection of irresistible words that you can possibly muster. A strong headline alone can dramatically improve your odds of success.

We've Become A "Headline Society"

Now that we're in the midst of the information age with a massive eruption of information coming at us from an infinite number of sources, the role that headlines play, has become even more significant in the grand scheme. We live in a "headline society". With free time becoming an increasingly scarce commodity, people use headlines as time-saving devices to direct their movements and attention.

Today's choices in terms of information, is at an all-time high. So many possibilities… so little time. It seems as if there's never enough time to be, to have, and to do, all those things we'd really like.

With available time at a premium, and the sheer volume of choices growing at a staggering rate, we place greater importance on spending time on things of interest and we filter out the rest from among the choices we're presented.

There's an overwhelming amount of material available for reading these days. Your message has to stand out, in order to get noticed.

For your headline to attract an audience and pull them in beyond the opening, it has to touch the prospect in a way that immediately arouses interest. By communicating specifically to your prospects about something of relevant importance, you provide a valuable service by helping them focus on issues of self-interest.

Headlines are enormously beneficial in all forms of print communications. They allow readers to instantly scan information for items of particular relevance and importance. As readers, we've all grown accustomed to using headlines for direction and guidance. So the opportunity to lure large audiences with carefully crafted, meaningful headlines is alive and well. And it's available to you.

Spending creative time to develop a compelling headline is one of the highest-payoff marketing activities you'll ever do. Your headlines are that important. They can make either a success or a failure of your ads, your campaigns… even your business. A good headline can mean the difference between a profitable outcome and a substantial loss. Do not overlook the pivotal role and enormous value of the headline.

The Most-Read Part Any Ad, Article, Letter, or Report

No words are read by more people than those contained within the headline. According to one of the top advertising gurus of all time, David Ogilvy, *"five times as many people read the headline as read the body copy."*

Headlines provide the necessary detail to help readers determine where to spend their time. They tip off readers and either attract or repel them in droves.

If your headline doesn't instantly reach out and "touch" the prospect, chances are good that the rest of your ad doesn't stand a chance. If the headline fails, the ad fails. The same holds true for written communications of all kinds -- sales letters, articles, brochures, newsletters, articles, press releases, yellow pages ads, web sites, order forms, catalogs, etc. Even the success of a non-fiction book is largely due the title -- which is essentially a headline boldly displayed on the front cover.

Headlines are the prime determining factor. The headline tells prospects whether they should *read on* or *move on*. With such a daily barrage of messages coming at us from all directions, from the moment we rise until we rest, it's not surprising that most of us only scan headlines with our filters operating at high capacity. Those filters can also be "blinders" that prevent even the best-targeted prospects from gaining the full benefit of your message. What this means is that your headlines have to work even harder to attract attention. The world is getting busier and more competitive all the time. Headlines that work are those that break through the barriers to reach their intended targets.

Your headline is the appeal that attracts hungry prospects. It dangles something of immense interest in front of a selected audience, where there's a good chance it will be noticed. The idea of the headline is to only give the reader a sample -- just enough to whet the appetite and stimulate the desire for more. Headlines attract prospects like candy attracts kids. If the appeal is attractive enough, it pulls in large numbers of readers. If the promise or offer isn't appealing enough, the prospect won't be lured inside.

What The Experts Say About Headlines

A few marketing experts were asked for their thoughts on the importance of headlines.

The question asked of these experts was this: *"How important are headlines in your view, to the overall success of written communications?"*

Following are the exact responses received.

From Monique Harris, author of, *"How To Successfully Sell Information Products Online"*...

"Can you imagine a typical 7-page sales letter with no headlines? What about a 6-paneled brochure? Talk about one big run on sentence! You'd never get anybody to respond to your marketing message.

Good headlines are like lampposts on a dark road. Done effectively, they help guide the reader from Point A to Point B, in a smooth and efficient manner. When done ineffectively, they cause the reader to get lost, and quite often give up the task of reading your materials.

That's why you'll hear so many top copywriters say they take several hours - (or days) - to create dozens of headlines, before choosing the perfect one. They understand how that a well-timed headline, can make or break the sale, in a matter of seconds."

Ken Silver, author of *"How To Make $100,000 A Year In Your Spare Time Creating Profitable How-To Manuals"* (www.ksilver.com) responded this way…

"Discover 5 little-known secrets that let you make a fortune on the Internet in less than a day!

Did this sentence get your attention? If so, you've discovered how a headline is the ultimate attention-getter. A good headline makes you curious, often by promising to reveal further information by reading on. There are many ways you can do this… but the most important is by placing trigger words in this sentence, such as "discover," "little-known," "secrets" and "fortune." These simple words, when used in certain combinations, are a powerful formula.

Not only do they attract attention and inspire you to read further, but they should also promise to reveal - in a tantalizing way - what might be coming next.

There is nothing more powerful than a good headline. It is a true sales tool… one that opens the doors to allow the sales process to begin."

And small business coach, Wanda Loskot (www.loska.com) had this to say:

"(Headlines are) extremely important. Some experts say that 90% of the effectiveness depends on the headline - that means that for every dollar you spend, 90 cents is invested in the headline. Funny thing is that usually people spend much more time creating and editing the body of an ad, letter, article, etc. - and the headline or title is just created on the spur of the moment. BIG mistake. If the

reader does not find the title interesting, intriguing, or at least...
annoying or controversial - he will not read the rest, most of the
time."

What Great Headlines Do

1) Get Attention

The first job of the headline is to capture attention. Your task as a
headline writer is to stop readers cold and get them to pay attention to your
message.

There are 2 factors that influence the attention-getting effect of
headlines: content and design. The content refers to the actual text used
and the design reflects how the words are presented in a visual sense.

The words you choose should cut right to the heart of your most
appealing message. Never beat around the bush -- you'll only lose your
audience. Instead, go for the jugular with words of paramount importance
to the carefully targeted prospect you're addressing.

Your headline should instantly communicate something that's of
vital importance or interest to your market. If your new invention helps
users save time or money, say so in your promotional headlines. If your
product makes a typical task faster, easier, or less of a hassle, use that
information in your opening. Whatever it is your prospect wants most --
that you can deliver on -- that's what you should present in the headline.

Capture attention with your most advantageous or most remarkable
claim or benefit. What does your product or service do that others don't?
What makes yours more valuable, special, or unique? How would the
prospect be better serviced or more advantaged? What is your greatest
benefit? A unique benefit that promises something the prospect deeply
desires but cannot get elsewhere, is a surefire attention-grabber.

For most applications, headline design is also an important factor.
One obvious exception would be classified ads where, in most cases, all
advertisers are provided the same size and style of typeface.

You want your headline to visually leap off the page, making it impossible to be miss. This is particularly important in display ads and directory listings like the Yellow Pages where your ad is competing all the other ads on the same page. With the Yellow Pages, you're in direct competition with neighboring ads, so it's even more important that yours projects a visual appeal that compels maximum readership.

2) Identify A Target Audience

Another important function of the headline is to single out the individual prospect you're most interested in addressing. You want to be sure that the folks you're communicating with are the best prospects for your offer, product, service, or business. To communicate with others is wasteful from a business point of view. And when you're talking headlines, you're talking business.

Ideally, your headline should telegraphically communicate to your chosen audience. If you want to reach bricklayers, but your publication is read by all the building trades, you need to make it obvious that your message is for bricklayers only.

Such a narrowing of the audience may be seen as limiting your potential. Nothing could be further from the truth. In effect, you heighten the interest among your specific target readership, while signaling to others that they shouldn't waste their time because this particular offer doesn't apply to them.

Singling out your prospects from the total pool of potential readers, is also known as "flagging". In essence, you're holding up a flag that says, *"This message is for _____ only"*. The blank space would be filled in by whatever market you're targeting. It could be athletes, women, plumbers, members of an association or residents of a neighborhood -- anyone of thousands of unique groups.

When you flag down your targeted prospects, you quickly gain their attention and interest because they immediately recognize your message as something that's specifically addressed to a group that they're associated with in some way. They could be convention planners, slow-pitch softball players, or hang-gliding enthusiasts... whatever group they feel a part of, any messages addressed to that group are recognized and given priority attention. After all, they're a member and therefore keenly interested in anything related to their membership

Messages that flag specific readers, cut through the clutter and by-pass the filters. They seem to speak to true prospects on a more personal level. These messages are immediately perceived to be of a higher value and significance.

You can use a direct or indirect approach to identify your audience. The direct approach could be something as simple as the pre-qualifier *"Attention Avid Fisherman"* or, *"A Special Message For Women Only..."* or, *"For Men Who Want To Retire Someday"*. In most cases, these identifiers are placed at the beginning of an ad, just before the main headline, although the last example, *"For Men Who Want To Retire Someday"* was a complete headline in itself that proved to be very successful several years ago.

The direct approach can also work as part of the text of the main headline. *"New Device Helps Farmers Monitor Soil Conditions Automatically With 100% Accuracy!"* In this example, the target audience is clearly identified within the words of the headline.

The indirect use of identifiers works a little differently. They imply that the message is for a specific reader. It's never as obvious as the direct approach and sometimes it takes a full reading to deduce the degree of relevance.

3) Deliver A Complete, Benefit-Packed Statement

Benefits, benefits, benefits. That's what everyone wants -- your prospects included. And, the bigger, more impressive, and distinctive the benefits are that you offer, the more powerful and fruitful your ads and marketing materials will be.

You need to clearly distinguish benefits from features. A feature describes what's in a product: materials, specifications, sizes, colors, etc. Features are product focused. Features are all those specific characteristics about a product.

Benefits are what each one of those features means to the prospective customer. Benefits provide the answer to the question that's forever on the mind of prospects *"What's in it for me?"* Benefits are the helpful advantages and solutions prospects get as a result of using or acquiring your product or service. Benefits are always 100% prospect and customer focused.

Benefits to the reader/prospect is all that matters to them. Specific, unique, hard-hitting benefits that stoke the fires of their deepest desires, or addresses their most painful anxieties. That's what every prospect wants: to satisfy a hunger or ease a pain. Give it to them in your headline and you'll have them as attentive and receptive audience members for the balance of your presentation.

Example of Features and Benefits

It's always a good idea to identify as many key features and benefits as possible before you begin the process of headline writing. Doing this gives you some powerful ammunition to use. Benefits have magical appeal to prospects and the more magnificent the benefits are, the stronger the appeal.

Let's take a look at a simple everyday product -- a 3-ring binder -- and see how we might identify features and then convert these into benefits. The chart on the next page shows examples of features and benefits.

Features	Benefits
4 inch rings projects	Large capacity storage for big
D-Frame ring construction	Holds 25% more paper -- up to 700 sheets plus, this unique frame makes for easy reading or studying as papers don't jam up like they do with regular binders.
Vinyl-clad, thick-gauge cardboard cover	Sturdy covers that last forever and can easily stand upright on a bookshelf for convenient storage.

Royal blue color - other choices available	Vibrant, attractive colors look great anywhere -- wide selection makes it easy to color-code your documents.
Chrome-plated steel rings	Nice, attractive smooth, shiny finish.
Easy-close levers at both ends	A perfect, precise close every time.
Sleeves on inside front and back covers	Great place to keep those extra documents and accessories.
Spine label pouch	Easily identify the contents of each binder – replaceable insert gives you the flexibility of unlimited use.

There are two important points to keep in mind as you consider various benefits to use in a headline:

1) **Place an emphasis on unique benefits --** those that others haven't stressed and preferably, something they can't compete with.

2) **Think like your prospect.** Empathize. Put yourself in your prospect's shoes and decide what benefit you (as a prospect) would most like to have. Can you deliver on that highly-desirable benefit? If so, be sure to use it in your headline.

Unveil your strongest benefits. Appealing headlines are about solving troublesome prospect problems through new, carefully conceived, quick and easy solutions. Since we're all interested in receiving helpful benefits, your headline should scream out specific, high-value benefits to your target market.

Present your benefits in a way the prospect can understand and appreciate. Strive for clarity. Be complete and compelling. Make it easy for any prospect to quickly grasp the advantages you promise.

Choose either a single benefit or a combination of benefits. Keep in mind that you want to add as much power to your headline as possible, so the more enticing the benefits, the more appealing the headline. Try combining a few, short, powerful benefits to create a stacking effect -- one that has more impact than each individual benefit alone.

Another technique is to blend together a bunch of individual benefits to create one "BIG BENEFIT". This is also referred to as the "ULTIMATE BENEFIT". The *big* or *ultimate benefit* is actually the cumulative effect of all those smaller benefits put together.

Here's an example of a headline that promises a big benefit: *"How You Can Make $87,000 A Year As A Successful Magazine Writer!"* The big benefit is clear -- it's how to make $87,000 a year as a magazine writer. Specific benefits might be… how to sell your articles before writing them… how to establish a relationship with editors… and how to gain an unfair advantage as a writer. Combine all three of these together and you have the ultimate formula… *"How You Can Make $87,000 A Year As A Successful Magazine Writer!"* (Steve Manning)

Always think about the buyer's benefits whenever you're in the process of writing a headline. When you're thinking from your prospects point of view, you're communicating on their level about something they are intensely interested in.

Immerse yourself in your market and learn all you can about their problems, frustrations, disappointments and desires. Then, present your ultimate answer to their dreams.

4) Entice The Reader Inside

Knowing your market is one of the keys to successful headline writing. When you fully understand what your audience really wants on a deeper level, you know what *hot buttons* to appeal to in your headline.

Misfire and your headline flops. But throw a strike and you could be blown away by the overflowing results.

When you know what your readers really want, it's easy to provide it. That is… as long as your product or service can deliver honestly and consistently.

It should be mentioned here that there's never anything to be gained by being deceptive. Use all the powers available to woo your prospect inside and to inspire action but… never, ever mislead anyone by promising something you cannot deliver on 100% of the time! Such practices will only hurt you in the long run. They could even spell the end of your business and land you in legal hot water.

Use your powers of seduction to arouse interest in your message. Curiosity can be a valuable tool when used correctly. Put curiosity to work in tandem with a strong benefit or an appeal to your prospect's self-interest.

Curiosity, used alone may arouse general interest, but rarely will it pull the targeted reader into the body of your message. It should always be directly tied to your product, service, business, offer, niche, or benefit. Capturing general attention for the sake of attention, is a futile exercise. No *general* audience is ever the best specific audience for whatever it is you're offering.

5) Hint At The Promise Revealed In The Body Copy

When the headline does its job, it compels prospects to keep reading. Good headlines tempt, tease, tantalize, or flat out make such a powerful and persuasive claim… that continued reading is almost assured. It makes prospects hungry for more and keeps them involved, absorbed, and filled with the hope of obtaining the promised benefits for themselves.

The benefit you suggest in your headline, is the major reason prospects will continue to read your ad or marketing piece. It's a magical lure -- that special something you've suggested could be theirs -- that captivates their imagination and compels prospects to read on.

Often a headline will merely hint at or give prospects a taste of what is to come. Often this mere sampling is enough to ignite a powerful desire that consumes the focus of the reader. And that's exactly what you want to do. Offer a sample -- a taste that makes prospects crave for more and urges them to seek out ways to get it.

For your promotional piece to succeed, you need maximum response. To achieve this lofty goal often requires every hook, crutch, and leveraging tool you can possibly find and then applying these to your headline. Remember… your headline is the most important part of your message. If you fail to attract sufficient numbers to keep reading, your headline is at fault and it's the first thing that needs to be revised.

What Happens When The Headline Fails?

Any headline that doesn't draw a large volume of interested readers is a failure and a detriment to the rest of your communication. When the headline fails, it diminshes the value of everything else associated with it – including your pitch.

You may have spent weeks developing an effective marketing strategy, designing an advertising campaign, or polishing up your complex sales letter. But it could all be a terrible waste of your resources. *If the headline doesn't pull them in, the rest of your work is irrelevant.* It's all for naught. A write-off. Completely useless trash. That's why it's so very important to make sure you've crafted the absolute best headline possible. If the headline is weak, the rest of your copy won't get read, your offer won't be acted upon, and you won't generate the sales you were hoping for.

Your effort, time and money will have been spent with little to show for it, if your headline doesn't deliver with impact.

Headlines play an important set-up role: they find an interested audience for your message and prime them for the rest of the presentation. It should arrest the attention and capture the interest of the largest possible number of qualified prospects.

Your best prospects are those who can benefit from your offer and are qualified to do so, meaning they have the ability to purchase your product or service.

Headlines Set The Tone

The opening you choose should set the stage for the remainder of your communication. Ultimately, it should communicate precisely what your message is all about. The headline acts as a title. It prepares the audience for what's coming and ideally, it should evoke an emotional reaction from the reader that makes him want to know more.

The tone is set by both the content and the look of your opening statement. You can adjust the tone, not only by changing the words of your headline, but by trying a different font, color, or design.

Good headlines address a definable audience and offer a promise of something better than what this particular group is used to seeing. The headline sets up a feeling of expectation, one that the body copy should naturally expand upon.

The Most Visually Dominant Text

As the lead-in to a document, headlines naturally attract the eye. Headlines set in larger type, stand out even more. Using large, bold type makes a headline the most visually dominant text component of your document or advertisement.

Ideally, you want your prospects to see the headline first. It's your best bet to attract an interested audience. The best way to do that is to offset the headline from the rest of the text, in some way. Since the eye is naturally drawn to larger objects first, it makes sense to increase the overall font size of your headline.

Understanding typical eye movements as prospects scan a page, can help you to design and position your headline for maximum readership. Generally, we scan pages from left to right and top to bottom. This is how we've learned to process printed information. Most of us have been conditioned this way. Don't fight it. Use this knowledge to your advantage.

We're naturally drawn to objects of color before looking to those black and white components. Darker shades catch the eye before lighter versions. We look at larger objects first, before moving on to the smaller details.

All this is done to help us digest information at greater speeds. We want to get the information as quickly as possible -- we want to comprehend the meaning instantly, in order to determine if we want to stay or go.

Here's a quick summary of the way most of us process printed information:

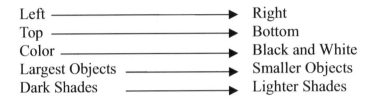

Left ⟶ Right
Top ⟶ Bottom
Color ⟶ Black and White
Largest Objects ⟶ Smaller Objects
Dark Shades ⟶ Lighter Shades

Want to achieve maximum readership of your headline? From a design perspective, you can start by using the above data. Start your headline at the top left side (or center) of the page or ad space. Make it contrast with the rest of the page by using a different color or a darker shade. Use larger type for your headline than the body copy. This can be used as a general guideline to help you incorporate a few basic design elements for maximum impact. A skilled graphic designer can create visual impact in other ways, but in most instances, these ideas will serve you well.

Your One Big Chance To Hook Your Reader

Just consider for a moment how you read a newspaper. You might be interested in World News, Sports, Entertainment, Finance, or Fashion. But once you've chosen a section, what's the next thing you do to find what you want? Chances are your eyes quickly scroll across each page looking for something of real interest to you. Everything else is simply blurred out. It's deleted from your range of focus. Your eyes zoom in on topics of interest to *you*, personally. Nothing else stands much of a chance of consuming your valuable time and attention.

What is it specifically that you scan, when you're looking for information of interest? It's the headlines, of course. Headlines help you determine where you spend your time and what you can avoid without a second thought.

It's the same scenario when you're standing at the magazine display in your favorite bookstore. First you find a section of interest. Next, you scan the covers waiting for a headline that calls out to you and beckons you pick up that particular publication.

Headlines are a great aid to help us select articles, reports, and advertising messages that each of us has an interest in. That's the key. Headlines that interest *you* -- pull *you* in. If the headline doesn't grab you, you move on to the next page, the next magazine or the next mail package.

With every headline that you use, wherever you happen to use it, you need to maximize its attention-getting power. It's your one big chance to gain the interest of your prospect. So it behooves you to use your absolute strongest, most alluring appeal. With anything less you're short-changing yourself by limiting the rate of response you can expect.

Headlines Tell Your Audience Why They Should Be Interested

Something about your headline has to capture the interest and imagination of your prospects. There has to be something there that jolts them and gets prospects to sit up and take notice.

You first need a solid understanding of your market and what it *needs* and *desires*. You've got to uncover that special something that your product or service provides that the marketplace currently isn't getting – yet desperately wants. Convey this *magic solution* in your headline and you're sure to raise more than a few eyebrows.

Headlines tell readers "at-a-glance" what the message is about. Each reader can then decide whether it's worthy of their time, or if that time is better spent elsewhere to satisfy a pressing want.

Headlines help to ease your audience into the heart of the message. But, effective headlines are never casual in their approach. You've got to serve up your most appealing promise, your most attractive offer, or your most provocative statement to draw prospects inside.

Your headline tells the audience what they can expect by delving further inside and what they'll miss out on by avoiding the message altogether. Effective headlines offer a reward for reading -- some kind of a payoff that's revealed in the body copy. It's the promise of this payoff that captivates readers and ensures that they stay tuned in.

Make it tempting. Add a little intrigue to heighten the curiosity. Make it inviting and welcoming. Offer the dream solution as though it's the answer to your prospect's prayers. Use whatever it takes to get your targeted audience interested enough to hear you out.

Summarize Your Benefits or Offer

Headlines work best when they convey the essence of your offer. Hint at the very best that's offered in the body copy that follows. Remember, it's the unique benefits and advantages that prospects are most interested in. Benefits stimulate emotional excitement and you need to generate that kind of energy and enthusiasm to enjoy maximum results from your marketing efforts.

Benefits are helpful solutions. They give the buyer an edge or advantage. Benefits make life easier or better in some way. Benefits are the answers prospects are looking for. Benefits add tremendous value to any product or service. In short… *unique benefits sell.*

Offers are those special deals or value packages designed to appear irresistible to prospects. Not in a sneaky way, but in a way that makes not responding seem like a ridiculous waste of a golden opportunity. Offers can include unique bonus items, premiums, discounts, one-time-only special deals, and the like. The combination of a powerful benefit and an appealing offer can make for a potent headline that really does the job.

Communicate What Sets Your Offering Apart From All Others

What is it that sets your product, service, idea, or business apart from the rest of the pack? What is unique about what you have to share? Take a different road. Try an original approach or an offbeat angle.

Headlines succeed when they focus not only on what sets the product or offer apart, but what gives it a magnetic appeal to the target market. Supply an extra advantage. Offer more. Make your benefits and your offer stronger than anything else the prospect may consider devoting time, energy, or financial resources towards.

Work at it until you find that Unique Selling Proposition or Unique Competitive Advantage. Emphasize any exclusivity – the "one-of-a-kind" value that you're bringing forward.

Without a Headline, There's Nothing That Jumps Out At The Reader

If you fail to use a headline, you're gambling that prospects will take the time to delve deep into your text to receive your full message. By doing so, you're actually making it more difficult for the reader. You're forcing readers -- your prospects -- to determine the meaning on their own.

In some cases, like a personal sales letter for example, you may choose to avoid the "typical" headline -- the kind that's positioned above the main text. In these cases, your first line actually serves as a headline that "sells" the reader on the rest of the message. So many of the ideas presented here could be applied with equal effectiveness to the first line of copy. But for the most part, you're better off to use headlines as powerful attention-getting opening statements intentionally set apart from the rest of the text.

Think of your headline as a brief commercial or ad for your total message. It's your chance to sell the reader on reading more and in so doing, fully expose him to your complete sales presentation.

Use your headline as a blatant attempt to attract the attention of your best prospects. Give it your best shot and hold nothing back.

You want your headline to figuratively leap off the page so your prospects can't miss it. If they do, all your efforts are in vain. If they catch your headline, and then choose to ignore your message, your headline didn't do an adequate job of *selling* your material to your audience.

Without a Headline, There's No Concise Summary... No Reason For Reading The Rest Of The Piece

A headline makes it easy for the reader to say "yes or "no". *"Yes, this is interesting to me. I must check it out"*... or, *"No, this isn't for me.*

Time to move on. "

Often the *yes* or *no* decision is made in a split second without the conscious awareness of the prospect. It's almost instinctive. Prospects have the ability to sniff out pertinent, promising, and valuable information… as well as the ability to see through and reject instantaneously the false claims, unsubstantiated hype, and weak, unmoving promises and offers.

If your headline isn't immediately clear, or if the information doesn't possess instant appeal, it makes it virtually impossible for the prospect to give it a "yes" vote and keep reading. Prospects know that most of what they see is worthless junk. Your job is to convince them otherwise. That's the duty of the headline… to quickly and convincingly plant a promising seed of possibility in the mind of your prospects. Compose your strongest, most powerful message and craft it into an easy to read and understand opening. Do this and you've got a winner.

Start using headlines throughout your materials. Use subheadings that stir interest while summarizing each individual section of a sales letter, article, or report. These headings help get your message across to readers who only check out the headlines as they skim through various documents.

Headlines are great lead-ins. They hint at the key information contained in the text below. They suggest the essence of the material that follows and allow the reader to decide future direction in a heartbeat.

If your message looks like a challenging read, most won't bother with it. It matters little what huge benefit you offer. You could have the ultimate secret -- the one that would lead them to land of opportunity and promise. If the headline provokes their interest or piques their curiosity, you've got an excellent chance of delivering your full message. If it falls short, forget it… you won't stand much of a chance.

A Headline Is a Tool Of Convenience That Makes Life a Lot Easier For Your Reader

Headlines are great time savers. They help the reader to make decisions -- decisions as to what deserves the undivided attention and what should be ignored. Therefore… most people like and appreciate headlines.

That's a clue. You'll never offend anyone by using a headline. In fact, to not employ a clear, descriptive headline is to short-change your readers.

As you read through this book, you'll probably find a chapter heading or two that appeals to you personally, more than the others. The same is true for every newsletter, book, magazine, newspaper, brochure, catalog, web site or any other document you come across. Specific segments are more appealing to you as an individual, and those are the ones that pull you inside.

Without the benefit of headlines or subheads, you wouldn't be able to quickly determine the relevance or degree of importance of each document or sub-section.

Headlines make it easy for the more general marketplace. Anyone who comes across your ad or receives your marketing material can decide whether the item warrants their attention and interest or not. This way you're actually providing a valuable service to everyone who is exposed to your message by saving them time and effort. Good subheads offer concise and intriguing summaries to help each recipient determine whether to *read on* or *move on* elsewhere.

Headlines Are Telegraphic Messages

The gist of your message should be revealed in the headline or subhead. It's okay to use a short, attention-getting or curiosity-arousing headline. However, if it's not followed up with a major benefit payoff, you'll quickly lose those readers you've tried so hard to attract.

You want the reader to understand the essence of your headline in the blink of an eye. There cannot be any confusion because if there is... you'll never get the results you're after in the first place.

Ideally, your headline should convey your main selling message instantly. By setting your headline in large type to clearly stand out, you actually direct your prospect's attention to it. This is your most concentrated and potent collection of power words in your entire document.

The headline that reveals a big idea -- *your ultimate benefit* or *huge promise* -- is the headline that signals to the true prospect that this is something of crucial importance. Your *ultimate benefit* is the reason they choose to stay. It's the thing that has captured the imagination of prospects. But the strongest of words can deliver with *greater impact and speed* when they are designed to jump right out at the reader immediately.

A Great Headline Makes The Rest of The Writing a Breeze

Developing a "killer" headline is just about the most important thing you can do as far as your marketing is concerned. But it's also very helpful in writing the rest of an article, marketing piece, sales letter, or display ad.

Headlines give you the optimum starting point and vital direction in the development of your copy, layout, and design. The headline acts as the lead. All you have to do is take that lead and run with it. Expand on it. Provide details. Explain it. Prove it. With the headline in place, you already have the best frame of reference possible. Now your copy has to follow through and deliver on the promise.

Creating a dynamite headline that's sure to capture an audience with its powerful impact will also give you an emotional lift and make the rest of your writing much easier. Once you know you've got a great headline, you'll be energized to see the project through to completion. The rest of the copy will be stronger and more persuasive as you feed off your awesome opening.

The Headline Is All That Most Viewers Ever See

Headlines are your first, best, and possibly, *only* chance to capture the attention and interest of the people you're aiming to reach. If five times more people read your headline than the body copy, *(a claim echoed by many advertising and marketing professionals)* than you've got to pull out all the stops to make your headline as inviting, interesting intriguing, or provocative as possible.

Most of the total audience exposed to any given message, never get beyond the headline. They haven't been "sold" on the idea presented, or it simply hasn't jumped out at them to attract their attention. There's no magnetic pull that captivates readers and lures them inside. That's the problem with most headlines: they simply lack pulling power.

Most people are busier today than ever before. There's more to get done. More to do. More to see. More demands and more pressure. And all of us are exposed to even more advertising messages daily than at any time in history. We're all bombarded with competing appeals for our attention, our interest, and our pocketbooks.

The only way to maximize readership and profit from the additional exposure of your complete message, is to hook more readers with a hard-hitting headline. The stronger the headline, the more readers will feel compelled to go beyond the headline, straight to the heart of your message.

Chapter 2

The Underlying Secret Behind Successful Headlines

Emotions Are The Key -- Here's Why

We're all emotional beings and as such, we respond to our feelings. As humans, we're intricately *wired* to respond to any emotional stimulus. Your prospects are no different. They react based on their feelings. Your prospects, customers, and audience members are primarily concerned about one thing and one thing only: getting what they want out of life *at that moment*. That's what they care about most. Give it to them and you'll be successful.

But there's a challenge you need to overcome on the road to success. You want to give your market what they want… and… you have the product to do it. But the task is a formidable one. You have to get your message across. You have to be heard. That is to say, you must effectively communicate your message to your market.

It doesn't matter how fantastic your product is. If nobody knows about it, you'll fail. Capturing attention and delivering your compelling message to your best qualified targets is what it's all about and the first -- and most important -- step to help you in your endeavor, is your headline.

So how do you ensure that your headlines capture attention and compel true prospects to further action? Answer: Appeal to the emotions of your audience. Emotions are the key. Find your prospect's *buttons* and push them into overdrive. Focus your headline efforts on appealing to the emotions. Find the *sweet spot* -- that point of power you know with absolute certainty is sure to trigger interest and intense desire.

Intellectual or logical messages don't stimulate responses. What induces response in large numbers are well thought out emotional appeals that almost force the interest of the reader, *even when it seems totally illogical to do so.*

Here's an example of an "intellectual" headline:

"Financial Strategies For Successful Retirement."

It's a straightforward statement. But does it move you? Does it inspire you to take any kind of action?

Let's add a little emotion to it. Here's a stronger version:

"Discover How You Can Retire In First-Class Comfort And Achieve Total Financial Freedom On Just $5 A Day!"

Think about your own interests and the kinds of appeals that get you to sit up and take notice. Do you respond with intensified interest when a basic emotion you already have is set off, leading you to want to know more?

As human beings we are literally driven by our emotions. It's impossible to separate those emotions from our thoughts. We attach feelings to everything including people... situations... messages... actions... and decisions. We're directed by our feelings. Keep that in mind as you work on your headlines. Rewrite your best headlines into new, more powerful versions. Put your heart into it. Fuel your passion as you write and you'll create headlines with unstoppable power.

Anyone exposed to your headline begins to make an immediate judgment about you and your product. It doesn't matter whether those judgments are accurate or fair. An instant decision is made, often without conscious awareness.

If your headline is ignored or passed over, you failed to emotionally *move* your prospect. If on the other hand, your prospect is pulled into the heart of your message -- you've touched a *nerve*.

There is nothing more alluring, appealing, or seductive than the headline that *speaks* to the prospect about something of crucial, emotional importance. Headlines that attract huge numbers of targeted readers, are those that get into the head and heart of the prospect by connecting with what the prospect is already thinking and feeling.

Headlines succeed when they naturally penetrate the barriers and go straight to that special place where prospects *live* on an emotional level.

It all begins with thorough research. You have to know your audience. The better your understanding of your prospect's emotional *hot-buttons*, the more likely you are to create a winning headline. Know what it is that motivates your audience with respect to your product... and then play that card for all it's worth.

Six Basic Motivators

Here are the 6 primary motivators of human action:

- Gain or Greed
- Love
- Self-Indulgence
- Self-Preservation
- Pride
- Duty

Which primary motivator would provide the strongest appeal for your product? Shape your headline to match. But use other appeals too as you see fit. Decide which of these basic motivations is most likely to get the maximum response. Remember, it's not enough to get attention -- you need to get your prospect interested and involved.

If you're selling a business opportunity or money-making information, the promise of *"Gain"* would likely be a major driving force of influence in that person's life. If you're selling natural disaster emergency supplies, *"Self-Preservation"* would be an obvious string to pull. If you're promoting a personalized coat-of-arms based on somebody's family name, *"Pride"* would appear to be an obvious *hot button* of choice.

Any emotional stimulus should focus on the immediate concerns of the audience. To get the results you want, you've got to touch the prospect's life and emotions. That's where your prospect is at the moment -- mentally and emotionally -- and this is precisely the zone your appeal needs to enter into if you want to make your mark.

Determine the best emotional appeal for your product and be sure to get through to prospects in an interesting and compelling way. Though there's no guarantee anyone reading your headline will read on, those that aren't moved by the headline surely won't. Disinterested prospects are quick to leave, with no intention of ever returning.

Headlines that work well do the following:

1) *Capture the attention of a selected audience*
2) *Stimulate emotional interest in the prospect*
3) *Arouse enough curiosity to spark further involvement and action*

Curiosity is an important element but it must be linked to something the prospect is already interested in. When your prospect's interest is aroused, he naturally wants to find out more. An element of curiosity can add fuel to the flame of interest and turn a mild fascination into a burning desire.

Following is a long list emotional appeals to help you identify the best approach for your headline. This list represents a wide range of the underlying reasons why prospects respond to individual appeals. These are the very things prospects want.

Discover what your prospects desire most and appeal to that desire in your headline. That's a proven method of writing a winning headline.

103 Appeals You Can Use To Emotionally Turbo-Charge Your Headlines and Magnetically Attract Lots More People

To make money

To save money

To save time

To avoid effort

To achieve comfort

To enjoy health

To live longer

To be popular

To satisfy curiosity

To gain pleasure or enhance enjoyment

To feel clean

To be praised and admired

To be in style

To satisfy an appetite

To own beautiful possessions

To attract the opposite sex

To be an individual, independent

To emulate others

To take advantage of opportunities

To get a surprise

To be successful

To make work easier

To gain prestige

To be sociable

To express creativity

To be efficient or more efficient

To protect oneself and family

To protect the future of a family

To be a good parent

To be liked

To be loved

To express a personality

To be in fashion

To avoid embarrassment

To fulfill a fantasy

To be up-to-date with the latest trend

To own attractive things

To collect valuable things

To satisfy the ego

To be "first" at something

To enjoy exotic tastes

To live in a clean atmosphere

To be strong and healthy

To renew vigor and energy

To get rid of aches and pains

To find new and rare things

To be more beautiful or attractive

To win the affection of others

To satisfy sexual desires

To bring back pleasant memories

To be lucky

To feel important

To gain knowledge

To improve ones own appearance

To be recognized as an authority

To enhance leisure

To have security in old age

To overcome obstacles

To do things well

To get a better job

To be your own boss

To gain social acceptance

To keep up with others

To appreciate beauty

To be proud of possessions

To resist the domination of others

To relieve boredom

To gain self-respect

To win acclaim

To win advancement

To seek adventure

To satisfy ambition

To be among the leaders

To gain confidence

To escape drudgery

To gain freedom from worry

To get on the bandwagon

To get something for nothing

To gain self-assurance

To escape shame

To avoid effort

To have safety in buying something else

To protect reputation

To "one-up" others

To avoid shortages

To relax

To avoid criticism

To protect possessions

To avoid physical pain

To avoid loss of reputation

To avoid loss of money

To avoid trouble

To prevent unemployment

To replace the obsolete

To add fun or spice to life

To be in style

To work less

To conserve natural resources

To protect the environment

To make others happy

To find love

To feel intelligent

To be benevolent

Once you know the best angle to take, creating a successful headline is much easier. If you want to stir the emotions… get *emotional*. Get fired-up as though you absolutely must convince your prospect that you have what he wants most. Add *passion… excitement… enthusiasm* and *drama* to your message. Write with the power of a *super-being…* as though you possess the ultimate answer to your prospect's dreams and prayers.

Try thinking of your headline as a miniature movie that must captivate the audience in order to succeed. Create the dream. Show your reader how easily it can be fulfilled. Be the wizard that supplies the magic and your headline will produce magical results… magic solutions…. and magic answers. New ways to accomplish tasks with no work… no hassles… no sweat. Easy ways to enjoy pure pleasure. Give prospects whatever makes them *feel* good about themselves and life in general.

If there is a universal "want" -- it would surely be to live the very best life that is possible. We all want to feel good with more pleasure and less pain. Any enhancement that helps us accomplish this universal desire is most welcome indeed.

The Right Mental Mindset For Creating Emotionally-Charged Headlines

To craft dynamite headlines, you have to be in an upbeat, positive state of mind. If you're feeling less than your best, you're not likely to come up with your most effective creative effort. Before beginning this important marketing task, take the time to clear your mind, refresh your body and revitalize your spirit.

There's an infinite number of methods available to achieve a state of mind that's conducive to generating provocative, emotional headlines. Find something you like to do and do it.

One activity that works well is exercise. Going for a run or bike ride seems to have a marvelous mind-cleansing effect. Try it and you'll feel energized and more vibrant as the oxygen flows and blood pumps. During physical workouts you'll find fresh ideas suddenly pop into your head. If you're ever stuck for a headline, don't waste time grasping at straws. Instead, get moving and new ideas and insights will begin to apear.

If you don't feel like heading outside, you can always do some stretching and deep breathing exercises. *(For more information on the power of deep breathing, see Unlimited Power by Anthony Robbins)* I find this works almost as well as jogging or bike riding. Find any activity that you enjoy and do it before you attempt to create your headline and the task will be easier and more fruitful.

Another powerful method for clearing the mind is meditation. Meditation allows you to relax and free your mind of all the stress, tension, and worry that you may be harboring at any time. If you're feeling stressed, you cannot produce your best work. No matter how busy you are, you'll generate a better quality of work if you only take the time to calm the mind and free yourself from the mental clutter beforehand.

Reading is yet another helpful activity because it exercises the mind and opens it up to new possibilities. Music is an excellent choice too. A favorite song can be both relaxing and stimulating. Play it in the background and you'll help to create the right mood for headline creation.

Sometimes all you need is peace and quiet. Perhaps starting your day an hour earlier will give you enough time alone where your mind can operate more efficiently. Know when your most effective time is. If it's early in the morning, this is the time to spend on headline generation. If you find yourself more productive later on, set aside an hour or two and get to work.

When your mind is clear and you're free of the daily pressures, ideas flow with greater ease and abundance. This is usually when your best headlines come together. Just begin. You'll be amazed how easy it is to write powerful headlines if you only stay with it long enough.

Chapter 3

22 Types Of Headlines For Unlimited Creative Possibilities

There Are Many Ways To Use Headlines To Your Advantage

Headlines can be used in a wide variety of instances and in equally diverse applications. Here is a list of some of the types of communications that can benefit from powerful headlines:

Sales Letters
Classified Ads
Brochures
Envelopes
Direct Mail Packages
Postcards
Door Hangers
Card Decks
Display Ads-- all types, sizes and venues

Ezines or Newsletters
Articles
Web Sites -- index page and every page of a site
Banner Ads
Email Messages
Forum/Discussion Board Postings
Signature Files
Blogs and Blog Posts
Auction and Sales Sites Like eBay
Web 2.0 Properties such as Squidoo, HubPages, Digg, etc.

Press Releases
Media Kits
Advertorials

Posters
Flyers
Fax Broadcasts
Hot-Sheets
Catalogs
Inserts

Surveys

Books, Manuals, Courses, and other Information Products
Audio Products
Video Products
Software Programs
Reports
Print Newsletters

Yellow Pages Ads
Radio And Television Ads
Bus Shelter/ Park Bench Advertising
Billboards

Advertising Specialties
Letterhead
Business Cards

Event Promotional Tools
Transit Advertising -- Buses, Subways, Commuter Trains, Taxi-Cabs
Point-Of-Purchase Signs
Vehicle Signs

Virtually every method of marketing communications can be substantially enhanced with the development of stronger headlines. In fact, I'd even venture to say that every type of communication -- business or personal -- could be harder-hitting… more direct with a powerful punch…

and much more effective in attracting a listening audience with a riveting headline.

Following are 22 common types of headlines with examples of each to help you understand where each might be used most effectively. Many of the examples have been borrowed from my extensive collection of direct mail, brochures, flyers, display ads, postcards, and the like. Several others were created "on the fly" to illustrate a particular headline type.

1) The Direct Statement Headline

The "Direct Statement" headline is a straightforward assertion or claim about your product or service. It's usually quite short in length and to-the-point. There's nothing subtle about it. The more effective direct statement headlines have the quality of being able to raise an eyebrow, or drop a jaw just a bit, to increase the chances of future interest and involvement. You want to strive for some kind of hook that makes prospects take notice of your statement.

The Shocking Truth About Becoming A Millionaire!

Gentle Dental Care For Adults, Kids And Great Big Babies.

5 Billion Dollars. It's No Accident. In 2 Days I Can Teach You How To Get Your Fair Share Of This Huge Opportunity. (Robert Allen)

$10,000. You Have Been Pre-Approved For A ScotiaLine Personal Line Of Credit With A Limit Of $10,000.

Discover A World Of Natural Beauty

The Best Chocolate Cake You Ever Ate (Ladies Home Journal)

Get Up To 1.25% Cash Back And Become Home-Free Faster.

Financial Strategies For Successful Retirement

7 Cents A Minute Any Time, Night And Day, To Anywhere In America!

2) The Question Headline

"Question" headlines act as involvement devices. A question often commands a reaction from the prospect, thereby involving him in your concept, idea or thought process. Questions by their very nature beg to be answered. However, the key to using this type of headline is to focus your question clearly on the prospect.

You need to ask questions of the prospect that make him want to read on to discover the ultimate answer. Questions that are of particular interest to a targeted audience, are even more involving for those readers to whom the message is directed. The purpose is to get the reader to quickly assess his situation or to start to think about his current condition. Involve them and they'll be drawn inside.

Do Fears Hold YOU Back? (Nightingale Conant)

Do You Feel Frustrated With The Money You've Been Making? (Jeff Paul)

Would You Like To Save 45% On Your Next Vacation?

Is Your Future Worth Ten Bucks? (Gordon Alexander)

What Would You Do If You Had The Money?

Will You Accept The Enclosed German REICHSBANK NOTE For 100,000 MARKS, With Our Compliments? (Robert Collier)

What Makes Some Companies So Successful At Pleasing Customers?

Often questions are used as the initial component of a headline to first activate and involve the reader. They're then followed immediately by a benefit statement or an offer, either as part of the main headline or in a subordinate role as a subheading. Once your prospect starts thinking about the question, even if for a brief moment -- that's the time to deliver a benefit-packed message.

Are You Paying To Much For Auto Insurance? Look Inside To Discover How To Save Hundreds Of Dollars.

What's The Key Secret To Increasing Your Income By 917% If You Don't Know, Read On. You'll Find Out What It Really Takes To Pull More Sales And Profits From Every Ad Or Sales Letter You Ever Use.

Serious About Making A Fortune In Mail Order? Here's How To Make $1,062,693 Selling Information By Mail! GUARANTEED... Or Your Money Back! (Don Massey)

3) The Testimonial Headline

"Testimonial" headlines work best when the comments you use are quite different from the other buyer feedback you see around. It's the actual words of a satisfied customer, so it carries the benefit of instant rapport and increased believability with new prospects.

"CARD Is An Integral Part Of My Day. I Couldn't Do My Job Without It."

"WalkFit Is The Best Thing That Ever Happened To Me!"

"I Paid This Marketing Genius $600,000 In One Year Alone, Because He Made Me $2,000,000. Now You Can Hire Him For Less Than 1/10th of One Percent Of The Amount I Paid Him." (Jay Abraham)

"I Was Desperate To Lose Weight. It Felt Like I Tried Everything And Nothing Worked. So, Naturally I Was Skeptical About The "SlimTrim Program" ...But Am I Ever Glad I Ordered It! I Lost 47Pounds In The First 75 Days And Have Kept It Off Since!"

Testimonials can also be used as part of a longer headline as these two examples show:

"Join The More Than 1 Million Canadians Who Have Said *Thank YOU Molly Maid*' Since We Started Cleaning Homes In 1978."

"I Lost 33 Pounds In 30 Days!" No It Wasn't A Diet. No It Wasn't Exercise. Read About A Miracle Proved By Thousands Of Users.

4) The Command Headline

This one is a directive used to get prospects out of their *comfort zones* by a giving a clear indication of what they should do now. The actual command component of these types of headlines begins with a verb. It's a direct call to action of some sort. *"Do This" "Stop Suffering From…" "Claim Your Free Pass…"* are a few examples of phrases that indicate a command.

"Speed-Reading Secrets Of The World's Fastest Reader™. Don't Spend Another Second Struggling To Keep Up With Information Overload -- Read This NOW!"

"This Is Your Window Of Opportunity. Open It."

"Select A New Career. Choose From Any Of Our 15 Free Booklets."

"Enroll Now! Try An NRI Course For 60 Days IN Your Spare Time."

"Go Fish In Your Own Backyard."

"Join Me And 5 Other Top New York City Chefs For An Evening Of Fine Dining For A Great Cause."

5) The How-To Headline

This format offers the easiest, and in many times, most effective approach to headline creation. All you have to do is begin with the words "how-to", and follow that up with a hard-hitting benefit, a string of multiple benefits, or any one of a number of combinations of benefits, offers, questions, etc.

The "How-To" technique is also an easy place to start the headline creation process. If you're ever struggling to find a good headline in a hurry, there's no more reliable approach than the "how-to". Try it and you'll see for yourself. It's also a favorite technique of some of the highest-paid, and most highly regarded professional copywriters.

Using the "How-To" combination, or simply, the word *how*, can turn a somewhat flat, uninteresting statement into one that pulls remarkably well.

Consider the following message.

Soil preparation can help your garden produce a more abundant harvest.

Now insert just one word and watch how this one word makes it far more appealing.

How soil preparation can help your garden produce a more abundant harvest.

Did you notice the difference? With the second variation, there's a promise of a payoff. It's not merely a statement, but an offer to reveal the information the reader would like to know.

"How To Promote Your Web Pages For Maximum Response!"

"How To Increase Profits In Any Economic Climate!"

"Discover How To Turn What You Already Know About Your Work, Hobby, Or Personal Interests Into A Million Dollar Information Products Empire!" (Anthony Blake)

"How To Cash In On The Mail Order Business And Earn An Easy $15,000 Per Month With Simple, Homemade Products That Can Be Automatically Re-Produced And Sold Around The World!"

"How To Deliver Exceptional Customer Service"

"How To Get The Exact Name And Address Of Every Man, Woman And Child Who Is Every Likely To Become One Of Your

Customers!" (Gary Halbert)

"How To Recruit, Interview And Hire The Right Person. A Step-By-Step System For Selecting The Best Person For Every Job."

"How To Have The Best Sex Ever!" (Cosmopolitan)

"How To Tease Him Mercilessly, Seduce Him Slowly, And Then Rock His World In Ways He's Only Dreamed About!" (Cosmopolitan)

"How To Manage Multiple Projects, Meet Deadlines And Achieve Objectives"

"How To Understand, Access And Use The Internet"

"How To Use Cheap Little Classified Ads To Make As Much As $10,000 Per Day!" (Gary Halbert)

"How To Play Music By Ear"

"How To Create Seminars And Workshops"

"How To Live Rich On Any Income!"

"How To Make An Ordinary Business Into An Extraordinary Money Machine!"

"How To Attract Clients And Make Money Online Cheaply, Effectively and Risk-Free 24 Hours A Day" (Mark Lengies)

Another alternate to the standard "how-to" headline is the "how you can" variation:

"How You Can Make $87,000 a Year As A Successful Magazine Writer!" (Steve Manning)

"How You Can Build Your Own Successful Direct Mail Business From Home -- Starting With Just $500!"

"Revealed: How You Can See The World For Free As An In-

Demand Travel Writer."

6) The Indirect Headline

The "Indirect" headline is supposed to arouse curiosity and interest to get the reader to read on. The intention is to tempt, tease, and intrigue readers enough so they continue reading. But in reality, it's difficult to pull off. This kind of headline is usually meaningless when left alone. It requires some other component, like a graphic, working together with the headline to be completely understandable.

If there's one format I suggest you avoid completely, it's the Indirect headline. This style of headline seems to break all the rules of good headline development. It isn't a clear, complete statement in itself. Indirect headlines meander like a stream through the countryside, never delivering that channeled, power-packed, direct hit that is characteristic of great headlines.

This technique is used quite often. But I suspect the failure rate is exceptionally high. It takes a highly-skilled writer and a strong concept to craft an Indirect headline that captures the attention and compels the interest of the right audience.

"10 Reward Dollars Are Waiting For You At The Finish Line"

"The Best Of All Worlds Is Waiting Inside."

"A Very Special Opportunity Is Waiting... AND IT HAS YOUR NAME ON IT."

As you can easily see by reviewing the above samples, most "Indirect" headlines leave a lot to be desired in terms of interest and appeal. There's no real attraction... no compelling reason to read beyond the headline.

All these examples offer is a general appeal that is at best, a weak attempt to snare attention. They leave too many questions -- questions busy prospects can't be bothered to answer.

In the first example... The headline makes no reference to what the reward dollars are for. Instead, the writer expects (or hopes) you'll take the time to figure it out for yourself. Who has time for that today? Exactly right. Nobody.

The second and third examples are much the same. A suggestion of something that's *waiting* for us, but... no clear indication as to what that something might be. These are weak appeals to the curiosity of the recipient and nothing more.

7) The Guarantee Headline

One powerful way to get attention is to use a strong "Guarantee" headline -- particularly a guarantee that's unheard of in your category or industry. Such a headline grabs the readers attention because the guarantee is so different that it jumps right out at the reader.

Adding a guarantee to a strong, benefit-oriented headline makes that headline stronger. If your guarantee is better than anything your competitors offer, or, if you feel safe in doing so, consider featuring it in your headline.

"Double Your Appointments In 30 Days Or I'll Pay You $500 Cash!"

"I'll Teach You How To Quickly & Easily Get All The Credit You Ever Wanted... 100% Guaranteed... Or I'll Pay You $50 For Wasting Your Time!"

"Project Management Guaranteed To Help You Complete Your Projects On Time, On Budget, And On Target."

"The 'Art Of Negotiating' Guarantees To Make You A Better Negotiator."

"Guaranteed New Techniques For Managing Stress, Reducing Anxiety & Staying Cool In Any Pressure Situation!"

8) The Frustration/Problem Headline

The "Frustration/Problem" headline works to establish rapport with the prospect by identifying, right-off-the-bat, a major pain the prospect is experiencing, that your product helps to resolve. The first step is to define the problem. Usually this is done in question format to involve targeted prospects. The benefit follows immediately afterwards.

You only want to remind your prospect of the frustration or anxiety he feels in order to establish a connection. No need to dwell on the problem in the headline… simply project your understanding of your prospect's plight. You want him to see that you're empathetic to the cause. Then, present your solution as the ultimate answer to his painful situation.

> "Paying Too Much For Poor Workmanship And Constant Delays? Fire Your Contractor NOW And Do It Yourself! It's Easier Than You Think With The Home Improvement Video Series By Time-Life!"

> "Tired Of Paying "Scalpers Prices" For The Best Concerts And Sporting Events In Toronto? Here's How To Find Out About Available Tickets To Every Major Performance, Game, or Special Event, BEFORE Anyone Else!"

> "If The Unexpected Happened To Your Computer Data Today… Would It Still Be "Business As Usual" Tomorrow? Here's A 100%-Guaranteed Way To Make Sure That Never Happens!"

> "There Were 63 Different Ways Thieves Broke Into Houses Last Year In Allegheny County Alone! Is Your Home And Family Safe? Call For Our Free Home Protection Kit And Enjoy Your Peace Of Mind."

> "Tired Of Those Cheap, Amateur $10 Haircuts? Now You Can Look And Feel Your Absolute Best Every Time With The Help Of Our 'Professionals-Only' Salon. Your Satisfaction Is Guaranteed 100% -- Or You Pay Nothing!"

9) The Deep Discount Headline

The "Discount" headline is a straightforward approach built around a special price, introductory offer, or an unbelievably low price designed to capture immediate attention. This technique is common among book and CD clubs. It can also be particularly effective in highly competitive retail markets such as electronics and clothing.

"Up To 30% In Insurance Savings And 15 Minutes Of Long Distance Calls FREE For One No-Obligation Call."

"Buy 100 Pens At 49 Cents Each And Get 100 FREE!"

"A Best-Seller Now Available For 25% Less!"

"4 Books. 4 Bucks. No Commitment. No Kidding. If You Love To Read, This Offer Is A 'No-Brainer'."

"12 CD's For The Price Of 1! No More To Buy."

"Take 6 Books For $1 (plus shipping and handling) With Membership."

"MILLION DOLLAR SECRETS: ONLY $19.97"

"It's The Cookbook Store's 10th Anniversary And To Celebrate... Here's Your 10% Off Thank You Coupon -- Good On Any Purchase Until Dec 31st."

10) The Personalized Headline

This technique is a surefire way to attract serious interest in your message. Nothing hits home like a communication that addresses the individual on a personal, first-name basis.

Few expressions are more attractive to anyone than the sound of his or her own name. Don't you naturally feel better about people who call you by name? It's like having a friend or trusted advisor sharing something they know is important to you.

This type of *callout* captures attention and heightens interest as the reader recognizes that this message is personally addressed, making it as relevant as can be. This boosts the message's perceived value in the mind of the recipient.

When you use the personalized approach you've got an audience that is listening to every word with their undivided attention, until they're either led to action, or their interest fades away.

"Robert Boduch Triumphs Once Again! Smart Pickering Resident Will Get A FREE, Financial Post Attache Plus Two Weeks Free By Starting Daily Delivery Now At A 37% Savings!"

"If You Have And Return The Grand Prize Winning Entry And Correctly Answer A Skill-Testing Question, We Will Be Pleased To Announce That THE RESULTS ARE NOW IN: Kelly Ann Boduch Has Won One Of Our Two $1,666,675 Prizes!" (Publishers Clearing House)

"Robert... Please Accept The FREE GIFT, Along With Your 50% Off Savings Voucher. But Hurry, This Voucher Expires June 20th, 2009."

"If You Would Like To Do Something Exciting and Yet, DIFFERENT For Allison's Birthday Party This Year -- Then Here's An Inexpensive, 100% -- Guaranteed Way To Do It With The Least Amount Of Hassles And The Most FUN!"

"Finally, Here's How You, Bob Boduch, Can Use 1,479 Of The Best-Kept Secrets Of The Worlds Greatest Gourmet Cooks And Impress Your Dinner Guests Like Never Before!"

"Top Marketer Mr. Robert Boduch Makes Brilliant Decision. Starts Own Subscription to Marketing Magazine at Over 50% Off The Cover Price."

You could also use a form of personalization to channel your message to an identifiable audience by virtue of their association with a specific group. Simply preface your headline with a "flag" that clearly identifies your audience and in so doing, magnifies the perceived importance of your words. This in turn leads to higher readership and better returns for you.

A Special Message To My Fellow Toronto-Area Firefighters... (Headline Follows Here)

Attention All Bay Area Cottage Owners…

Nudists!…

Formula-One Racing Enthusiasts!…

Attention Detroit Real Estate Professionals!…

11) The Benefit Headline

Virtually all headlines should contain at least some form of benefit. The exception being a headline that's designed solely to stop readers in their tracks… before delivering the benefit payoff. When a strong benefit isn't part of the main headline, it should immediately follow it as the sub-heading or opening line of copy.

The trick with a simple "Benefit" headline is to come up with the ultimate advantage for your audience. It's this attractive benefit that people want and if you can give them something they crave, something they hunger for -- they'll be more inclined to maintain their focus on your message and take action on your offer.

Simple, concise, Benefit headlines work well in display ads of all sizes, where you may not have as much space to use longer headlines like many of the examples you'll find throughout this manual.

"Yes YOU Too Can Learn To Create Beautiful Crafts With Ease!"

"15 Ways To Help You Qualify For The Job You Want"

"The Secrets Of Successful advertising By Mail."

"Make An Unforgettable Entrance and 15 More Ways To Focus Everyone's Attention On You" (Cosmopolitan)

"50 Idiot-Proof Ways To Make Money On The Internet!"

"Tips Tools, And Tactics To Boost Your Online Sales By Thousands Of Dollars!"

"43 Tips For Smooth, Sexy Skin" (Redbook)

"$11,600 A Month With Tiny Classified Ads! You Can Do It Too, Once You Discover These Inside Secrets!"

"Experience The Kind Of Profoundly Pleasurable Sex Most Men Only Dream About!" (Prevention Health Books)

"Financial Strategies For Successful Retirement."

"Sexy Hair In Minutes" (Redbook)

12) The "Reasons Why" Headline

The "Reasons Why" headline can work well because it promises to reveal some important information the prospect needs to know. This technique usually begins with a specific number and lures prospects in with an approach that arouses their curiosity.

People love to know the answers and a "Reasons Why" headline promises such answers. It's almost a challenge to the reader -- to learn these reasons and compare them with his own ideas and beliefs.

"7 Reasons Why You Should Choose Pro Window Installers Over All The Others"

"3 Reasons Our Boxing Day Sale Is The Only Electronics Event You Need To Attend All Year Long!"

"47 Invigorating Reasons To Enjoy First Class Pampering At Our New Luxurious Spa And Resort On Lake Of The Bays."

"9 Reasons Why You Should Visit Us Before May31st."

13) The Short Headline

On occasion, a headline of one to three words may be just the thing you're looking for. Although short in length, this kind of headline can still pack a wallop through with a direct message and visual presentation that cannot be missed.

"Short" headlines are best used in small display ads where space is at a premium. In most cases, these ads are surrounded by many other ads all calling out for the reader's attention.

In the case of the Yellow Pages, those other ads are often from direct competitors, so grabbing attention with a short headline is even more challenging. The best way to make these headlines stand out is to simply magnify its size. Make it as big and bold as you can. A visually dramatic headline jumps right out at the viewer as soon as the page is reached.

What If...

**That Faint Cry For Help You
Thought You Heard Last Night,
Actually Came From YOUR Child?**

Body copy goes here. This is not actual copy
Body copy goes here. This is not actual copy
Body copy goes here. This is not actual copy
Body copy goes here. This is not actual copy
Body copy goes here. This is not actual copy

The idea of the Short headline is to capture the eye of the preoccupied prospect. These headlines seem to break all the rules of good headline writing except for that one. They command attention largely due to the effective use of relevant words set in the oversized type.

The best headlines also cut through with a carefully targeted word or phrase. The headline *"Rupture?"* spoke directly to hernia sufferers and was instantly recognized as such. And it proved to be a tremendously successful approach for a company that offered medicinal therapies.

Any further compelling details should be placed in the follow-up text -- those words that run right under the headline. This includes benefits, offers, guarantees, or anything else you would consider placing in a longer headline.

"If Only…"

"Rupture?"

"Wet Bed?"

"Millionaire Secrets!"

"Oh My God!"

"Gosh!"

"Wham!" (Herschell Gordon Lewis)

Amazing Mileage Multiplier! (Jerry Fisher)

Find Help. (Jerry Fisher)

Wife Wanted. (Singer Sewing Machines)

Sheesh!

14) The Case History Headline

This headline illustrates through actual examples, the kind of results prospects can reasonably expect. That's the implication, anyway. Through a summarized story, readers are provided with a true picture of actual, measurable results.

This type is very similar to a testimonial headline. The information is basically the same, but, the delivery may be different. Where Testimonial headlines are a first-person account of an individual's genuine experience, case-histories are often expressed in a third-person format. It's the true story of an actual experience or result. The difference is that this story is told by someone else, from their perspective. It's similar to how a journalist would cover a story with their own interpretation, delivered in a hard-hitting, concise way.

> "Starting Off With $56,000 In Debts… A Young Divorced Mother Tells How She Became A Millionaire In Only 34 Months. Here She Explains How You Can Start Earning Enough Money – Easily -- Working At Home, to Retire A Millionaire In 5 To 10 Years."

"You Can Start With Less Than $100 And Make Lots Of Money With Classified Ads! I Did, And I'll Teach You How!" (Melvin Powers)

"The Amazing Story Of The Frustrated Librarian Turned Millionaire Property Developer Who, Started With A Single Home And Amassed A $5,000,000+ Fortune In Less Than 10 Years!"

15) The News Headline

Most of us are interested in news of some kind. New discoveries fascinate us. If *news* of a general nature lacks appeal, news that relates to individual preferences, biases, and personal interests, is always worthy of attention from that particular type of person.

The key again is in targeting. Target your "News" headline so the message is seen as crucial, must-have information of value.

Press releases are the most common application of a news-style headline. But *news* can also work in many other ways.

"A Surprising New Discovery For Those Who Always Suspected They Had The 'Right Stuff' To Succeed In Their Own Businesses… But Who Haven't Quite Got Going."

"Ex-Marketing Director Of International Publishing Giant REVEALS Priceless 'Trade Secrets' That Have Been Kept Under Wraps For Years!"

"Announcing A Captivating New Collector Plate Presented By The American Society For The Prevention Of Cruelty To Animals."

"Everything Else Has Gone Electric To Save You Time And Money. Now We've Done The Same For Postage!"

"Here At Last Are The Unspoken Sexual Health Secrets You'll Never Hear From Your Doctor. Your Husband. Your Wife. Or, Heaven Forbid, Your Mother!"

"The World's First Personal Postage System. Never Run Out Of

Stamps Again!"

"Doctors Astounded By The Possibility Of These Miracle Self-Healers!"

"Car Saved By Massive Transfusion"

"100% Uncensored Sex Survey-- 3,500 Guys Confess Their Raunchiest Romps, Most Mortifying Moments, And Biggest In-The-Sack Freak Outs." (Cosmopolitan)

16) The Numbered Headline

This technique features a specific number as an actual reference point. It's similar to the *"Reasons Why"* headline in this regard. But the number can actually reflect many unique points such as the number of secrets a book reveals, or the number of ways your customer is greater advantaged by using your product or service.

"Numbered" headlines work well because of their specific, numerical reference. An exact number appears much more credible and believable to the prospect than any average or rounded-off number ever could.

"47 Idiot-Proof Ways To Train Any Dog In Just 30 Days!"

"The 7 Secrets That Can Make YOU A Better Speaker."

"13 Secret Marketing Tools That Will Help You Build Your Business, Gain More Free Time And Put More Money In Your Pocket Every Week!"

"9 Steps To Sponsorship Success. What To Do... And When To Do it. 32-Page Guide FREE When You Subscribe."

"6 Ways To Make Your Site Search Engine Friendly" (Monique Harris)

"12 Symptoms You Must Not Ignore" (Ladies Home Journal)

"New Video Unveils Secret Push Button Site That Contains...

20,139 TARGET MARKETS - All You Do Is Punch In Your Keyword. It Spits Back Product Ideas, Target Markets, and Back End Ideas. What's more, It Tells You How Many Products Were Sold, At What Price Point, Percentage of Men vs. Women and even HOW They Were Sold, So You Don't Have To Reinvent The Wheel. (Marlon Sanders)

17) The "Not This -- But This" Headline

This approach is designed to clearly and decisively distinguish your business, product, or service from the rest of the pack. By identifying what you are not first, you create a unique position -- one that's very different from all the others.

"No MLM, No Chain Letters, No Pie In The Sky Schemes, No Recruiting, And No Get Rich Quick Scams! Proven Strategies Anyone Can Use To Sell Any Business, Product Or Service Online To Generate Extra Cash Flow On A Weekly Basis!"

"No Annoying Reply Cards. No More Pressure. No Unwanted Shipments. Now, Start With 12 CD's Free!"

"No Horoscopes. No Fashion Tips. No Perfume Strips. Just Smart, Clear Financial Advice For The Independent Woman." (Jerry Fisher)

18) The "If... Than" Headline

This technique outlines the problem to be solved, the goal to be reached, or another pre-qualifying statement *before* delivering the details of the payoff. It's a proven strategy to remind the prospect of the problem he'd like to overcome -- before delivering the ultimate solution in the same statement. This helps to clearly focus your reader on the message as he anticipates the details of your proposed solution.

"If You Have A Good Driving Record, Better Insurance Rates Are On The Horizon..."

"If You Qualify... You And 5 Friends Could Be Off To A Week-Long Ski Vacation In Vermont!"

"If Your Home Is Plagued By Ants, Earwigs, Roaches, Or Any Other Creepy Pest, We Can Quickly And Easily Eliminate These Annoyances Forever With Our Automatic, Bi-Monthly Fast-Blast Service! It's Guaranteed 100%!"

"If You Would Like To Write Your Own Best-Seller And You're One Of The First 75 To Respond To This One-Time Offer, You'll Not Only Learn The 21 Steps To Becoming A Winning Author... You'll Also Get This Huge FREE Bonus Kit Worth $979.00 To Jump-Start Your Own Success!"

"If You Want To Lose 10 Pounds, Comfortably, In The Next 3 Weeks, Gold's Health Club Can Help You Do It In Just 30 Minutes A Day, 3 Times A Week -- 100% Guaranteed! Only $29 Dollars When You Book Your 1 Month Special Before March 15th! And... There's Never Any Obligation To Continue."

"If You're Really Serious About Making A Fortune In Mail Order, Here's How To Make $1,062,693 Selling Information By Mail Guaranteed... Or Your Money Back!"

19) The Invitation Headline

This headline format is straightforward and right to-the-point that works best with personally addressed direct mail. An invitation is a soft-sell technique that often flies under the radar. This approach is more likely to be accepted by the recipient, if he hasn't been hit with it before.

"Invitation" headlines imply a selected audience. The more effective it delivers this perception of exclusivity, the more success you are likely to experience using this technique.

"A Remarkable Invitation To Enhance Your Life, Ben! (For Michigan State Alumni only)"

"You Are Cordially Invited To Take Advantage Of A Very Special Offer From The Financial Post."

"You Are Invited To Join Our Grand Opening! Sneak Preview For

Our Local Customers Only. Shop Early And Save An Additional 15% On Red Tag Sale Prices!"

"You Are Personally Invited By Raymond Aaron To Attend A Very Special Event…"

20) The Offer Headline

"Offer" headlines are focused around a limited promotion. It could be an introductory price, free trial, sample, or any kind of package deal. These headlines work best when the offer clearly represents outstanding value.

But value alone isn't enough. Whatever you're offering must also must be something the prospect is interested in acquiring. If he's already thinking about it when your special offer comes to light, you've got a good shot at grabbing a ready-to-buy prospect.

The "Offer" headline is similar to the discount headline. However, unlike the Discount approach, an Offer headline doesn't necessarily have to directly relate to a product's purchase price.

"Get Your Hands On A FREE Trial Issue Of FAST COMPANY. You'll Never Let It Go."

"Examine Any Book Free For 15 Days."

"Do Not Pay For One Full YEAR On A Huge Selection Of Home Furnishings, Home Appliances And Home Electronics! NO INTEREST. NO DOWN PAYMENT. Plus, We Pay The Tax!"

"This Book Is Invaluable, Indispensable… And It's FREE!"

"Try The NRI Writing Course Of Your Choice For 60 Days -- Risk Free! See Details Inside!"

"Here's A Special Opportunity To Reserve An Advance Copy Of Canada's Most Powerful Business Intelligence-Gathering Tool. To Take Advantage Of This Pre-Publication Offer Please Reply By June 30th."

"To Us You're As Good As Gold! Presenting A Rare 2 for 1 Opportunity…"

21) The "Attachment" Headline

This one is a little different in that it always has some unusual item physically attached to the message. Actual attachments could be anything --a small piece of string, a poker chip, a novelty item -- any one of thousands of different toys, gadgets, trinkets, or samples. It's use is primarily in direct mail packages -- although attachments could also ride along with brochures, postcards and door hangers. The idea is that this seemingly odd item makes any piece stand out from the rest of the daily mail... and getting noticed is half the battle.

It is perhaps the single most dramatic way to get your prospects to pay attention to your message: to have something unique attached to it. This approach has worked well for me and other marketers and has become a personal favorite for getting a hig rate of response. Almost any attachment will get noticed -- and the package opened -- a key first step in any direct mailing. Attachments add bulk, giving your mailing a distinctly different feel, one that invariably triggers curiosity.

The secret to making your attachment work advantageously is to choose an item that is the perfect match to your headline. Often with this technique, you'll decide on the attachment before writing the headline. What you need to remember is this: *the headline must be obviously connected to the attachment, or the result will be confusion.* And confused prospects rarely read on and they never buy.

One of the first examples of this type of headline was *"The Penny Letter"* written by Robert Collier, which had a bright shiny penny attached to it, with the headline *"It's A Marvelous Thing - The Power Of Money To Make More Money!"*

Another early example came from Reader's Digest. This one used two bright and shiny pennies, displayed through an envelope window, bearing the headline, *"If Thou Hast Two Pennies…Spend One On Bread. With The Other, Buy Hyacinths For The Soul."*

Here's some additional examples of attachment headlines:

Attachment: Set Of Dice

Headline: "Why Gamble That New Business Will Come To When You Can Almost Guarantee It?"

Attachment: Gourmet Coffee Packet

Headline: "Sit Down, Have A Delicious Cup Of Coffee On Us, And Discover How You Can Enjoy This Fresh-Roasted Colombian Coffee -- Every Day!"

Attachment: Miniature Screwdriver

Headline: "Having The Right Tool At The Right Time Ensures A Successful Outcome."

Attachment: Bag Of Microwave Popcorn

Headline: "For Copy That Just Pops Off The Page… Call Me!"

Attachment: Abacus

Headline: "This Is An Old-Fashioned Way Of Doing Accounting. For The Newest, Most Efficient, And Cost-Effective Accounting Services… Please Call Me!" (Jerry Goodis)

Attachment: A Slice Of Fresh Berry Pie

Headline: "I Know You Want A Bigger Slice Of The Pie. I Can Help You Get It." (Jerry Goodis)

Attachment: 2 Small Pieces Of Yarn -- one red and one blue

Headline (This actually appeared as the opening line of a sales letter): "Just Two Little Pieces Of Yarn -- But What An Important Story They Tell You."

The letter continued with the following copy...

"Pull the ends of the red yarn and notice how the strands separate and fray easily. Now, pull the blue yarn and notice the difference -- it will not fray!

The red yarn was spun by machine; the blue yarn was spun by hand in far off Persia."

22) The Combination Headline

So far, you've learned about several different types of headlines. Here's another twist that gives you infinite possibilities for headline ideas that can work for virtually any form of communication. This method is a powerhouse. In fact, the right mix can produce an avalanche of response.

The "Combination" headline is nothing more than a mixing or combining of two or more of the other headline techniques. The end result of several combinations is a hybrid version that has even more attention-getting and interest-arousing capability.

Here are a few different combinations. See if you can identify the various headline techniques that are used.

"What's The Key Secret To Increasing Your Profits By As Much As 917%? If You Don't Know, Read On. You'll Find Out What It Really Takes To Pull More Sales And Profits From Every Ad Or Sales Letter You Ever Use."

"Free Video Tape Reveals 11-New Ways To Make Huge Amounts Of Cash... Even During A Recession. Discover The Key To Making Money Anytime, Anywhere... And Take Control Of Your Finances Forever!"

"Do You Have What It Takes To Succeed At Your Own Business? This Free Book Will Help You Find Out. YOURS FREE! Starting Your Own Business... 12 Steps To Success!"

"Now You Can Easily Double Your Income By Learning The Insiders Secrets Of The Most Successful Self-Publishers In The World… and I Guarantee Your Satisfaction! Plus… If Act Now, You'll Also Get Valuable FREE BONUS Tools Worth $299!"

"Busy? Want Ideas That Work? Invest 20 Minutes Per Month In Your Career. You'll Get More Than 100 Communication Tips And Techniques -- Ideas That Will Help You -- And Your Staff. You'll Get More Done Faster, With Less Effort And Resistance. Guaranteed Or Your Money Back!"

Whatever type of headline you choose, make sure it's as strong as it can be and that it's the right fit. A long combination headline, or a lengthy testimonial is often better suited to a full page magazine ad or sales letter… as opposed to an article, small display, or classified ad.

A short, direct, big-benefit headline has the advantage of casting a wider net. But this may or may not prove to be the most successful from a marketing point of view.

That's why testing is so important. Make your headline as powerful as it can be… and then test it.

Try a different variation. Add another element to create a combination effect. Or, line up 3 strong benefits in a row and stack one on top of another, creating an irresitible urge in the prospect's mind. Consider the medium itself, available space, your chosen format and the intended result. Each can impact how you proceed in selecting a suitable headline.

Take as much space and use as many words as you need for maximum impact. Make sure that when you edit or shorten your headline, you don't weaken its power in the process.

There's often no clear line of demarcation separating the various headline types. For example, a *Command Headline* may also qualify as a *Benefit Headline*, and many different formats could also be used as *Attachment Headlines*. Some headlines could actually be placed in various categories. Create headlines from each group, but don't get hung up on trying to categorize them. Various headlines are provided here to simply spark your own creative efforts.

Chapter 4

What Do Great Headlines Promise or Offer?

Guarantees

It's difficult to argue against a strong guarantee. You've already seen a number of headlines that featured guarantees. Every prospect has a certain degree of fear in dealing with an unknown supplier. Anything you can do to alleviate that fear, both real and imagined, can go a long way towards boosting your bottom-line results.

Guarantees are something that many consumers have grown accustomed to. It's almost something they take for granted. Most assume a kind of guarantee is available, whether this is indeed the case or not. Many people expect to be able to return products to their source, should they be discontented with the results achieved.

But a guarantee that carries impact is one that gives the prospect a perceived feeling of absolutely risk-free involvement on their part. When you have such an iron-clad, risk-reversal type of guarantee, than it deserves to be featured in your headline.

1) Guaranteed Results

While guarantees vary, the strongest ones promise some kind of impressive results. These kinds of guarantees are powerful because the results are easily measurable by the customer, in most cases. The stronger your guarantee, the more it becomes a powerful tool in convincing the prospect that there's really little to lose by taking the requested action.

Common examples of guaranteed results are offered in smoking cessation and weight loss programs. *"Stop Smoking In 30 Days Or Pay Nothing!"* is a typical example that doesn't use the word "guarantee" to convey a strong "results or else" message. *"Lose 10 Pounds In 2 Weeks... 30 Pounds In 30 Days -- Guaranteed!"* clearly states the promised benefit and adds power by guaranteeing the same results. The nature of the guarantee is not disclosed, nor is it as forceful as it could probably be, but the mere mention of the word *guarantee* adds believability to the claim and a degree of credibility to the organization.

Results can be promised with a variety of products, services and offers. The promise of *"A Greener Lawn – Guaranteed!"* (Weal and Cullen)… or *"Fresh, Hot, Delicious Pizza Delivered To Your Door In 30 Minutes, Or It's Free!"* (Domino's) certainly removes risk from the action proposition presented to prospects.

Guaranteed results give customers a yardstick from which to gauge their own results. A specific, quantitative promise makes it easy to monitor the actual results achieved when the proposition gets put to the test. It allows buyers a point of comparison -- it's a measurable goal -- it's something prospects want and now they have a means to verify the claims you've made in your presentation.

Guarantees offer an obvious payoff; they melt resistance by helping to overcome the prospect's fear when venturing into the unknown. They project a level of confidence suppliers have in their own product and this confidence is transferable to prospects and customers. The assumption is, if the product wasn't up to the promise, the supplier wouldn't be guaranteeing it.

2) Money-Back Guarantee

The strongest form of a guarantee is the complete *"money-back guarantee"*. Some even go beyond that by offering *"double your money back"*, or… *"your money back plus a free bonus"* just for trying out a product. The advantage of the money-back guarantee is that it helps prospects overcome their natural reluctance to… A) believe your story… and… B) take action on your offer.

The money back guarantee provides reassurance and comfort to the prospect. Knowing that their purchase is, in effect, insured with a money-back pledge, helps dissolve the perceived risk. They feel that their money is protected by your full guarantee.

This type of guarantee can be used anywhere. It's particularly effective with new products or services, new companies and unknown names. Promotional material for information products like books, manuals, audio recordings, DVD's, and software programs… can all be made more effective with a risk-free guarantee. The same could be said for a wide range of general merchandise and services.

Any new product, service, or business, should strive to provide a powerful, money-back guarantee as part of an arresting headline. Anything "new" in the marketplace has additional hurdles to overcome as prospects are even more leery of yet-to-be-proven products and companies. A money-back guarantee can go a long way towards alleviating any fear of loss a prospect may have.

The stronger the guarantee, the better. A 90-day guarantee typically beats a 30-day guarantee hands down… and a 12-month guarantee is better than one that's only good for 6 months. The more heavily your guarantee favors the prospect in terms of available options and risk management, the more effective it will be as a lure. The stronger the guarantee, the more value it adds to the appeal of your offer and the more it deserves to be part of your headline.

Office Depot, the large office supply warehouse offered a *"155% Low-Price Guarantee"*. Here's how they explained it: *"It's this simple: Find your purchased item for less and we'll match the price, plus give you 55% of the difference -- INSTANTLY! And we'll take your word for it!"*

Don't stress the guarantee if it's not vastly superior to what your competitors are offering. The same old, expected guarantee doesn't have the *"stopability factor"* required of headline copy. But a guarantee that blows away all competing guarantees by a sizable margin, gives you a powerful advantage to use in your headline.

Instant Gratification

There's no payoff like an immediate payoff. As prospects, we all seek solutions that offer the greatest dividends, at the lowest cost, in the least amount of time. It's all about "instant gratification" -- your market wants the reward, NOW and they're willing to pay a premium to vendors who promise quick results. Yes, prospects want benefits, to be sure. But preferably, without any waiting. Call it human nature, if you will. We're always looking to save time, energy, and effort. We all want those things that bring us fast results -- without the need to get off the sofa.

If your product or service promises rapid solutions to time-consuming alternatives, you have a great angle to use in your headline. Again, it must be stressed that your quick-fix solution has to be uniquely different from the other options available to prospects to make your offer stand out head and shoulders above the rest.

What kinds of descriptions offer instant gratification? Following are some examples excerpted from various headlines:

"Stop Smoking In Just 10 Days!"

"Rub Your Wrinkles Away!"

"How To Create Your Own Info-Product In Three Hours Or Less!"

"30 Days To A More Powerful Vocabulary!"

"In Just 10 Minutes, You Could Have Your Electronic Version Of The Greatest Direct Mail Secrets Of All Time!"

New, Improved Alternative Or Solution

Anything "new" that relates to your market is naturally of interest to everyone in that group. Prospects are forever looking for new and better ways to do things. If you've got something new to offer, stress that fact in your headline.

You could capitalize on the built-in appeal of new products and solutions by providing:

- upgrades to existing items
- new and improved formulas
- additional options that previously were unavailable or expensive "add-ons"
- variations of methods, services, or processes
- a brand new -- never seen before -- product or service

Anything you can offer that provides an improvement of some kind, or an upgrade, is reason enough to use this angle in your headline. Prospects are interested in anything that offers them more benefits than what they're already used to. Any improvement on an existing product that makes life easier, happier, or more successful, is likely to garner plenty of attention.

Offer an alternative solution to a problem that plagues your market. Make it more appealing in some way. Add additional value to the typical solutions that are available in your market.

What is it about your product or service that makes it the superior choice in the marketplace? Is it a real or perceived improvement over other options available? Is it a faster alternative? Does it simplify a process... save time, effort, or money... add comfort, convenience, or beauty? Is it easier to use or to assemble? Does it offer fewer hassles, or less maintenance? Is it bigger, smaller (if that's a perceived advantage), available in multiple colors, sizes or finishes, Is it more powerful? Does it use less energy? Will it last longer and provide extra value? Is it sharper... safer... more environmentally-friendly?

Whatever it is that you can offer... a unique advantage over the others... anything that provides a *superior solution* over the known alternatives, may be the edge you need to use in your headline for maximum appeal. What makes your solution the better one? That's what you need to be thinking about when you're working on your headline.

Often a more favorable choice is nothing more than an upgrade of an older product. Look at products on the shelves of your local pharamacy. There you'll find goods that are "*new and improved*", "*extra-strength*", and "*900ml for the price of 750 ml*". These are all attempts to gain an additional edge and boost sales by offering newer versions with added perceived power or value.

An Easy Way To Try-Out a Product

Another common headline approach is to make it very easy to get the product into the hands of the customer. Often a sample can be the most effective way to *sell* prospects on the benefits of ownership.

When you make it apparent in your headline that it's easy for anyone who may be interested, to take your product for a test-drive, you increase interest. If your product or service is something that must be seen or experienced to be fully appreciated, than this idea can work very well in your headlines.

How can you go about offering prospects an easy way to try out your product or service? Free samples… free trials for a limited time… trial subscriptions or sample issues… free software that's only accessible or functional for 30 days. All are introductory offers various marketers have stressed in their headlines.

The lure of anything that's both *free* and of significant *interest* to your prospects can be too much for genuine prospects to resist. Try it and you'll see for yourself just how effective this strategy can actually be.

"Secret" Information

The appeal of "secrets revealed" has been very effective when used in a headline. It's that highly-regarded "inside" information -- something that only someone with access to important details could provide. It's a case of supply and demand. There's a lot more people who lack this information and would dearly love to get it than there are people with the inside track to the prized knowledge of the ages.

Think about a topic you have a great deal of interest in. Something you do that you'd really like to do better. Lets say you're an avid gardener. Now… what if I could show you my "*7 Simple Secrets To Bigger, Juicer, More Delicious Fresh Garden Tomatoes*!" Wouldn't you be interested in this information?

Getting the "inside scoop" on news of interest is enticing because of the perceived advantages it will, in turn deliver. We all want to know the "trade secrets" in order to do something more effectively or magically. Gaining the inside secrets gives us an edge; a special advantage that no amount of practice or study is likely to provide. No wonder covert information can be so appealing.

Link your valuable information to an authentic source. A well-known name can provide strong supporting evidence and boost your credibility. Associate your source of information to a proven success for an instant credibility boost.

Another approach is to add a dash of mystery to the presentation in order to trigger curiosity and increase interest. Our natural curiosity causes us to be interested in mysterious or unusual findings. We want to know more and feel fortunate indeed to happen upon the piece that suggests an off-beat solution or remedy from an unlikely source.

This strategy is often used in the alternative health field where new remedies are being discovered and older ones, practiced by specific groups and cultures for ages, become more widely accepted and used.

Here are a few examples:

"Ancient Egyptian Concoction Promises Fast, Effective Drug-Free Relief From Stomach Cramps."

"Miracle Medicines From The Ocean Floor!"

"Hearing Loss? Try Immediately This Yoga Practitioner's Yawning Exercise."

This approach works well when you have ample statistical proof in your body copy. Often it pulls in readers because it's original and the answer is often surprising and intriguing.

At times, it almost appears "too good to be true". But we're driven by our nature to look for new and better solutions, so we become captivated by the spell of a mysterious connection.

Something Of Vital Interest To A Specific, Targeted Audience

Headlines that appeal to specific, identifiable groups are the most successful of all. One major function of the headline is to select a specific audience from the entire pool of possible recipients. It's unlikely that everyone is a genuine prospect for your offer, unless you're conducting a highly-targeted direct mail campaign.

Whatever it is you have to market, it will only be of interest to certain people and only and for specific reasons. This is the audience you should address exclusively. Forget everyone else. Focus your attention on true prospects and create your headline to call out to these people only.

Prospects choose what to pay attention to based on headlines. It's the first statement readers see that either attracts them, or send them packing. The headline has to appeal to your individual niche market. You've got to strike the right chord in order to capture readership.

Prospects decide at a glance what they'll direct their attention towards and they look to the headlines and graphics to quickly make their decision. If you fail to win them over at this point -- you've lost them forever.

What's most important to your specific market? If you market to folks who like to go fishing… how to land the big one-- a prized catch, would likely have magnetic appeal. Try to work this kind of pulling power into your headline.

"Attention Salmon Fishermen Fed Up With Gimmicks, Fancy New Lures, And Expensive Gadgets: Derby Champion And Private Tutor To Serious Anglers Reveals 5 Simple But Powerful Insider Secrets For Catching Bigger Salmon – More Often!"

If your market is woodworking hobbyists, what would they most like to know? My guess would be, tips on creating professional-looking furniture and crafts from home.

"Easy-To-Learn Secrets Of Master Cabinet Makers! Discover How The Pros Make Those Difficult Cuts And Create Perfect Joints Every Single Time!"

Try to isolate ONE THING your audience would most like to have. What benefit are your prospects in search of the most? Effective headline creation begins with a thorough understanding of your market. Know what they want and what you can deliver.

Gain an understanding of your specific market and it's preferences, biases, likes, and dislikes. Good headline writing demands a comprehensive understanding of the target market and the deeper the understanding, the easier it is to sculpt a winning headline.

Get inside your prospect's mind. Discover what he's thinking about. What are his likes and dislikes? What would he most like to be, have, or do... and how can you connect that desire to your product or service? What's on his mind?

If your product were the answer to his prayers, what would it also do or provide? Can you adapt your product to accommodate this desire? How is your prospect most likely to find out more about your type of product or service? What group does your prospect belong to? What publications do they subscribe to?

Know your reader and you'll discover an appeal that works. Discover what prospects like to read and where they hang out online and you'll know how you can reach them.

Believable Results With Actual Figures

Actual numbers add believability. Headlines that quote real numbers (authentic-sounding figures that represent verified results) have the capacity to deliver with greater impact.

Here's an example of a general headline for an investment course. *"Make More Money In The Stock Market."* It offers a benefit -- making more money from the markets. But how much is "more"? Who knows? Could this headline be made more effective? You bet! And the way to do it is through actual numbers.

Here's a better alternative:

"Make 23% On Your Money Every Year With 7 Simple, Time-Tested Stock Market Secrets!

Mentioning average returns of *"23%"* certainly has much more appeal than *"make more money"*. It's an actual number. It's real… something prospects can quickly grasp and understand. It provides a base line -- something that's possible for the prospect to attain with the help of this program.

The second change *"7 Simple, Time-Tested Stock Market Secrets"* suggests that these methods are both little-known (secrets) and… have been used repeatedly (time-tested) – and put to the ultimate test in the real world of harsh realities. Also, the fact that there's just 7 secrets, makes it seem more easily achievable.

Using actual numbers adds a degree of realism and believability to your claims. Actual numbers give prospects something they can relate to. It's a measuring stick. Prospects can compare their current results to those promised in your headline. This approach causes prospects to imagine the possibilities with the kind of thought that says -- *"hey... maybe I can get this kind of result too!"*

Chapter 5

Techniques and Strategies For Creating Headlines That Work Every Time

The Starting Point of Great Headlines

Following are several tips to help you get started developing a winning headline from scratch:

Prepare first. Do your research. Begin by identifying 5 key elements: your target market… the product or service you're promoting… the most appealing benefits your product or service offers… your prospect's major frustration… and what special inducements you could use to encourage more interest.

Learn all you can about your audience. Understand why this audience will be interested in what you have to offer. Ask yourself, "What's the single, most-compelling reason a prospect should choose me, my product or service vs. the competition?" Determine the best medium to reach prospects and uncover the strongest, most compelling promise you can make about your product or service.

Envision your typical prospect as you write your headline. Create a composite of the type of individual you want to address and keep this image in the back of your mind. This strategy will help you develop a headline with reader-appeal – one that enables the prospect to imagine himself getting the same kind of results your headline promises.

Investigate all aspects of the product or service thoroughly. Look at it in different ways and from unique perspectives. Often potentially explosive, fresh, headline material lies hidden-- just waiting to be discovered.

Assess the competitive environment before constructing your headline. You want to create a headline that's likely to contrast with all others vying for the same audience. If all competing messages are screaming loudly for attention, take an opposite approach and whisper.

Find an unusual edge, a unique angle that you can ethically exploit and turn into promotional firepower. Find something competitors aren't using that you can boast about.

Consider possible barriers, objections or marketplace challenges and provide a solid explanation. What obstacles does your headline have to overcome? Is there a major hurdle or misconception to clear about your industry, company, product or service?

Talk to your existing customers. Get to know them. Find out the underlying reasons why they bought from you. This will help you make the right emotional connection with new prospective customers -- the kind of connection you want to establish with your headline.

Collect headlines that capture your eye or attract your interest and save them. You'll find my collection of headlines included in this manual. Study successful headlines from the past and write out several of these by hand, before attempting to write your own headline. This technique gives you the unique viewpoint of the original writer. Warm-up with this little exercise and you'll be giving yourself a definite advantage from the start.

When you're ready to start writing headlines of your own, you might want to remember these important points:

Clear your mind. You cannot create your best work if you're busy thinking about a dozen other things. Begin with a calm, relaxed mind, a positive attitude, a glass of freshly-squeezed juice, or, if you prefer, a cup of fine coffee, and a fresh pad of paper.

Launch your headline project with a blank pad of paper and a list of key words related to your business, audience, product, service, and the unique advantages that set you apart. Next, try writing a straightforward claim about how the prospect will gain from whatever it is you're offering.

Be prepared to invest plenty of time into headline development.
Examine several possibilities. Try different word combinations. Experiment. Be prepared to rewrite and revise. Eventually you'll evolve a potent collection of words that will work well as a headline.

Think Benefits

It's always a good idea to take the time to completely uncover and articulate each and every possible benefit from your product or service. After all, it's benefits that attract attention and the more impressive the benefit, the more attention you'll draw.

Every product, every service, every business, has multiple features. Features are specific qualities that are built into a product or service. They're all the details that pertain to products, services, and business. Features include colors, sizes, functions, ingredients, materials used, hours of service, etc. Everything about your product or service itself, is a feature. What those features mean to prospects and customers are benefits.

The best way to derive powerful benefits is to first list every conceivable feature. Jot down every thing you can think of. If your product is something you can place in front of you as you do this exercise, so much the better. With a service, try to think of everything you can about that service.

Create a list of features on the left side of a page, or... write each individual feature on a single 3 x 5 inch index card. Now with each feature, transform it into a powerful advantage to the customer. What does that feature mean to the end user? How will they be advantaged by this feature? What's great about it from the prospects point of view?

Turn each feature into a benefit with magical appeal. If you created a single list on half a sheet of paper, use the other half to write out each corresponding benefit. If you used index cards, use the opposite side to record the benefit of that feature.

Creating a complete list of benefits gives you tremendous leverage and a huge head start in headline writing. Each benefit could actually be converted into a headline. But not all benefits have equal appeal in the marketplace. Your task is to decide on most compelling benefits and focus on those exclusively, for your headline. You could combine several benefits to either create an ultimate benefit or a multi-layered benefit package. *(For more on this, refer to the "Combination Headline" section of Chapter 2)*

Since prospects are most interested in benefits, you'd be well-advised to give them what they want. In so doing, you're appealing to their self-interest. The more accurately you can identify, appeal to, and provide what they intensely desire, the more successful you'll ultimately be. Generally speaking, headlines that don't offer a benefit, explicit or implied, don't often fare well in the marketplace. In fact, it usually means "farewell" to a marketers dollars in record time, with little or nothing to show for it.

Benefits fuel emotions and emotions drive human behavior. They make it easy for prospects to assume the result for themselves; to play the role and achieve the promised payoff. The more effective you are in transferring those benefits to the imaginary experience of the prospect, the more likely you are to keep that prospect interested and to get him to act on your offer.

Benefits are the answers people are looking for. Focus on benefits. Make them big, bold and original. It's your best bet at capturing attention and interest.

Here are some examples of benefit headlines taken from my collection:

"Business Writing For Results! Make your words sizzle with the clarity, impact, and power that gets results."

"For Less That $500, You Can Get Into The Profitable Business Of Car Detailing And Earn $55 Per hour Or More!"

"37 Tips, Methods, And Techniques To Help You Increase Your Daily Site Traffic By Thousands Of Visitors."

The "Ultimate" Benefit

An "ultimate benefit" is the result of several individual benefits, all stacked up to create a giant benefit. It's a combination of major advantages designed to create one all-encompassing benefit that has even more appeal and power than any single benefit alone.

The *ultimate* or *big benefit* is a compilation, or the assumed end result of a collection of individual benefits. Let's look at an example.

Think and Grow Rich, by Napoleon Hill, has been a best-selling book for decades. The title, I'm sure, has played a large role in the success of this book. It's an ultimate benefit headline, one that promises what millions want -- how to *"think and grow rich"*. Nowhere in the book does it tell you … *"think this and you'll get rich."* But if you were to apply the specific benefits contained within it's 13 chapters, you would, in effect have all the necessary tools to tap the vast powers of your mind to create a future of abundance.

What's the underlying dream solution your prospects want and you can provide?

That's essentially what an ultimate benefit delivers. It's a *miracle cure* and *the answer to a deeply held desire* that has yet to be fulfilled. An ultimate benefit stimulates the imagination and takes the prospects away to some far-off dreamland where his ultimate fantasies and burning desires are realized.

Here's another example:

"Experience the kind of profoundly pleasurable sex
most men only dream about!"

Hmmm. That's quite a provocative statement -- something I'm sure would interest millions of men the world over. What makes this promise an "ultimate benefit" is that it represents the *optimum desireable result* in the minds of the target market.

Multiple Benefits

Another way to add extra power to your headline is to string together a series of strong benefits. This usually works best in 3's. "Get this benefit… and this benefit… and also this benefit…" has a more compelling effect than any individual attribute. Plus… sometimes it's difficult to chose one benefit over another. One prospect reacts differently from the next. What *grabs* one may not mean much to the next person in line. Multiple benefits gives you added punch and a better chance of capturing and conquering the audience.

Below are some examples of multiple-benefit headlines:

"Sink your teeth into taste so rich and luscious… you'd never guess it's low-fat! Live the food-lover's life and still lose weight. FREE FOR 21 DAYS!"

How To Win Tons Of New Customers, Get Them To Buy More Often, Increase The Dollar Amount Of Every Sale, And Double Your Profits In Record Time!"

"Prestige, versatility, a minimum credit line of $10,000… and now a special complimentary bonus."

Understanding Human Nature

Being aware of what drives human behavior can help you write more successful headlines. When you know what makes people tick – and your market in particular, you're halfway there to finding a headline that will reach out and touch them.

Most people only care about themselves. If you write headlines that talk about you or your product -- you're missing the mark. You'll never attract an eager audience that way.

But if you tell them how wonderful their life will be because of their intelligent decision to acquire your product, you'll quickly gain an interested and attentive audience.

What it all boils down to is communicating in a way that will produce a favorable result and that means communicating in a language your prospect can fully understand and relate to. Give them what they want. Tell them what's in it for them. Put your words together in such a way that keeps the reader interested.

1) People are filled with hope.

Most of us hope for a brighter future. We want things that make us feel better. We forget that we control our feelings independent of outside "things". The desire for an imagined "thing" which is essentially the pleasurable feelings associated to a product, builds such emotional intensity that it overrules and dominates the mind. It's impossible to separate the feeling from the thought. So the more intense the feeling becomes towards a product, the more desirous the acquisition of such a product becomes.

Your prospects have wants, hopes, and desires too. But they've been let down before by other promises which didn't quite measure up to the promises. And so most prospects have become a little jaded… cynical about promises and claims. They consider it nothing but hype. However, their hope lingers on. They're emotional beings who truly want those benefits and they feel cheated when they don't get them.

Whatever grandiose claims or promises you make… you must also be able to deliver on with your product or service, or you'll never be able to experience long-term success.

2) It's difficult to resist something *interesting* and *free*

The power of a strong free offer, has been proven countless times by marketers of all kinds. "Free" is a great incentive to get people to take action. But always connect any free offer to something of relevant interest to the audience you're targeting. *Free* plus something of perceived value and significant interest equals great response. "FREE" can be a powerful headline word for the right kind of offer and market. Use it effectively and you're chances of success soar.

3) People generally like to reciprocate

What you give is what you get back. According to spiritual law, it's impossible to give without it coming back to you in some way. In a practical sense, when prospects are given something of value free of charge, they not only appreciate it but feel compelled to give something back. Often this takes the form of a purchase.

This concept of reciprocation is explained in detail in the book, *INFLUENCE The Psychology Of Persuasion* by Dr. Robert Cialdini. The key here is to reach *genuine prospects only.* Don't waste your time on others. Real prospects are worthy of the best offers your can develop because the perceived value of the freebie is higher and it's appreciated when the gift given is a perfect match for the audience.

4) Nobody likes to be misled

Use all the tools in this book and others to create the most appealing, compelling copy you can possibly imagine. But… never, ever short-change prospects on the promises you make.

Communicate with clarity. Build the desire of prospects and get them to take action. Just make sure you come through on all claims made. One dissatisfied customer can cause you enough grief to drive you out of business. Make sure that whatever you say and do is not only true, but also *appears to be true*. Perception is everything. Understand this at the outset.

Arouse Curiosity

Have you ever read a headline that consumed you with wonder to the point where you couldn't wait to find out what it was all about? Headlines that pique curiosity, cause the reader to stop for a moment and ponder. The more the prospect thinks about it, the more inclined he is to seek out the answers. And the only way to do that is by reading the balance of your copy.

Curiosity-arousing headlines can often pull in huge numbers of readers. But huge numbers won't mean anything to you unless these people are targeted readers for your message or qualified prospects for your product or service. That's why it's pointless to use curiosity exclusively to get attention and to attract readership. Curiosity should be linked directly to a product or service benefit, in some way. And the link has to be obvious to any first-time reader. You can't expect your audience to interpret your meaning. It must be spelled out clearly without any confusion.

Here's the formula for using curiosity in your headlines:

Curiosity + Self -Interest = Compelling Appeal

Curiosity can add a magnetic pull to the appeal of your headline. But it must be used correctly if you are to achieve desirable results from its use.

Used alone, curiosity can draw large crowds. But in most cases, those crowds aren't the least bit interested in the product being marketed. They were lured by the headline and the interest that it generated. Not by the products or the benefits those products offered. So attracting large, but uninterested prospects will obviously do you no good whatsoever.

The way to use curiosity effectively, is to combine it with an element of self-interest. Curiosity, by its very nature, raises questions -- questions that beg to be answered. The mystique and intrigue is amplified, however, when the questions are particularly important to the reader. That is to say when the questions have something to do with the readers own personal interests.

You can add an element of curiosity by asking questions in your headlines or posing challenges to your prospect. Questions invite responses. Questions involve the reader -- but only to the extent that the subject matter is relevant, important and interesting. Otherwise, prospects won't bother to find the answer because *curiosity* was misused.

When the reader of your headline recognizes the topic as being of interest, he's already hooked, at least partially. But with the addition of a curiosity-arousing element, the prospect interest becomes intensified and he's pulled into your message with a heightened desire to find the answer because it could be very important to him.

Here's some examples of curiosity-arousing headlines that work because they're combined with self-interest and delivered to a targeted audience:

"MIRACLE MEDICINES You Can Make For Yourself In Just Minutes Using Every Day Ingredients You Already Have In Your Refrigerator, Your Pantry, Or Your Garden!"

"Tiny Ads That Can Literally Make You Rich If You Only Apply This Little Secret I Learned From One Of The Best Ad Writers Of All Time!"

"Do You Close The Bathroom Door Even When You're The Only One Home?" (Psychology Today)

"How I Went From Sweeping Floors To "Cleaning Up" As A

Successful Franchise Owner."

The combination of *curiosity* plus *benefit* is a powerful one. Prospects are always looking for benefits. It's what most of us have in the back of our minds as we involve ourselves in the activities of the day. It's as though prospects are equipped with radar devices that allow them to find what they're thinking about. Now... take the biggest benefit you can and add an unusual twist, or a surprising connection to pique prospect curiosity, and you've got a one-two punch that's a sure knockout.

The curiosity factor often hints at a solution -- sometimes from an unusual source. It tempts, teases, cajoles, and lures prospects to find out more. It's the teaser that gets readers hooked so they're pulled into your presentation.

> *Warning*: You must follow through and deliver a payoff in your copy. No one will keep searching indefinitely for the answer. Give them some kind of payoff -- quickly... and then build on that to continually fuel the prospect's desire.

Curiosity for the sake of curiosity will never give you a positive result. Always use a tie-in to whatever it is you're marketing. Curiosity alone has the potential to attract more readers. But many readers attracted by this approach aren't representative of the kind of audience you want to address. When you talk about specific benefits, you immediately appeal to your definable segment of the total market. It's as if the ears of your true prospects have perked up. You have their attention. Now add a little mystery... a little intrigue... something that will compel your real prospects to find out more. That's the most effective way to use curiosity.

Use Proven Techniques

When developing your headline, begin with the tried and true approaches that have worked for others. Try out the various ideas presented in this book. They all work to varying degrees in many different situations. When you've exhausted these proven techniques and strategies, then and only then should you try to get creative.

Empathy is one quality shared by great headline writers. According to the Collins English Dictionary, empathy is *"the power of understanding and imaginatively entering into another person's feelings."* It's the ability to get inside your potential buyer's head in order to communicate with words that are interruptive… have instant impact… and immediately consume their full attention. When a headline truly projects empathy and establishes rapport, it becomes something that cannot be ignored.

Following are two famous headlines written by legendary copywriters, that exemplify an empathetic understanding of the target audience.

"At 60 miles an hour the loudest noise in this new Rolls-Royce comes from the electric clock" (David Ogilvy)

"They Laughed When I Sat Down At The Piano But When I Started To Play!~" (John Caples)

Addressing a specific audience is another key ingredient of effective headlines. When you call out to a certain, definable individual -- you speak directly to that person. They recognize your message as something of specific importance because it's directed at the group that they're a part of.

Always think in terms of benefits to your readers. Tell them what they want to hear, give them something that will help them and you'll gain their attention.

Write As Many Different Headlines As Possible

One way to be sure to come up with at least a few headline gems is to create as many different headline possibilities as you can. The best way to do this is to start first with your list of benefits.

It's easy to come up with headlines that are based on a benefit. Try it out. Take a benefit -- any benefit -- and turn it into a headline. Then… simply create variations on those headlines. Try a few multiple-benefit headlines. If your original benefit list contains 10 benefits, these ideas alone can help you easily generate 30 or more possible headlines.

Next, try writing different types of headlines. (see Chapter 2) Start with one headline form each category. Try them all, if you can. For some, like "Testimonial" headlines, you'll need additional details. But for most others, like the "Question", "How-To", or the "Reasons-Why" headlines, you can quickly create multiple headlines. Let you mind go and see what headlines you can produce. You may surprise yourself.

Expert copywriters like Ted Nicholas (author of *Magic Words That Bring You Riches* and several other books, and other information products) and Brian Keith Voiles (author of *Advertising Magic*) suggest that you write out 100 headlines or more for a single ad, sales letter, or promotional piece. That number may seem a little intimidating. It's only a suggestion -- not a hard and fast rule. Just start writing. Let it flow. Try out the ideas presented here and you'll come up with a winning combination. Of this you can sure.

Here are some additional ideas to help you get started. Try using a list of keywords associated to your product, service, business, benefits, features, offer, or guarantee. Begin with the word in mind. Then state what's interesting or appealing about that. Think from the mindset of your prospect. Focus your ideas as though you were the prospect. What would appeal to you? (For more details on this method, see the "Brainstorming Technique" detailed in Chapter 7)

Study The Masters

Look at successful headlines from other sources as well as this one. Study the work of experts such as: *Victor Schwab, David Ogilvy, Maxwell Sackheim, John Caples, Dan Kennedy, Herschel Gordon Lewis, Bob Bly, Clayton Makepeace, Gary Bencivenga, John Carlton and Eugene Schwartz*, to name a few. My suggested reading list appears at the end of this text. It's a great place to expand your knowledge, not just on headlines, but on all aspects of copy writing.

Another way to become an excellent headline writer is to analyze those pieces that arrive in your mailbox. Review all the direct mail, postcards, sales letters, brochures, flyers, catalogs and every kind of piece that fills your mailbox. I've done this very thing for about the past 10 years and I've accumulated an extensive collection that includes all types of mailings and the headlines that were used on each. Some headlines are pure dynamite. But sadly, most are of the weak, poorly-developed, money wasting variety. But these too reveal valuable secrets for the avid student to capitalize on.

You can tell that a headline is effective when you start to see it again and again. I have in my personal collection, several packages that were sent to me on more than one occasion. With one package, I received no less than five identical solicitations from the same source, addressed to me personally, over a span of several years. No mailer in their right mind would mail a piece repeatedly like that, if it wasn't pulling in a reasonable profit. Any package that continues to show up over the years is a guaranteed money maker. And it's difficult to conceive of an effective, money-making direct mail package that isn't first introduced with a arresting and compelling headline.

Pay attention to the mailers, billboards, TV commercials, and radio ads that capture your attention. Make a note of the introductory words or headlines used. This is a good clue as to what works on various audiences. Sure, every market is different and requires a custom-tailored solution, but, basically we're all human and deep down, many of our wants are the fundamentally identical.

Think Of Your Headline as a Two Second Commercial

Your headline is an *advertisement* for the rest of your copy. It's the thing that must reach out to prospects and mesmerize them in a way that says, *"tell me more"*. But here's the clincher: you've only got a few short seconds to deliver the goods and make such an immediate splash, that the prospect continues to read and hopefully, to act on your proposition.

It's as though you wanted to advertise your restaurant to drivers on the nearby highway. As your potential customers round the bend, they notice a billboard on the horizon. When they get a little closer, your ad comes into focus temporarily. This gives you a tiny window of opportunity to convey a message that works. You need to motivate visitors to take the next exit so they can stop at your diner.

Take too much time, and your words are missed completely. Present a message that requires thought or analysis, and you've lost all hope of attracting prospects. Deliver a message that has a mixed meaning and you'll only confuse people. The only way your headline does its job is when it conveys your greatest promise or strongest benefit in the shortest, yet most compelling way possible.

Now…the time factor varies between applications, certainly. A

1/6th page display ad that's surrounded by other ads vying for the same reader's attention, must deliver instantly. A printed sales letter might have slightly more time and space to deliver it's power-packed opening, although it needs to be equally effective.

When you think of your headline as a billboard, you realize the important role it plays. It's your one chance to seize the prospect's attention and win a reading of your full message. You need to make an immediate impression with as much attention-grabbing power as you can possibly elicit.

Stand Apart With Your Most Unique, Competitive Advantage

What unique advantage do you bring to the table? You need to capture that uniqueness and express it in a way that has the most significance in your prospect's life.

If you promise the same as your competitors, there's no clear and distinct advantage to doing business with you. Whatever it is that gives your product, service, offer, or message an element of distinction -- as long as this distinction is perceived as an advantage -- should become the focus of your headline.

That's the thing that sets you apart. It's your edge in the marketplace, your competitive advantage. If you can't find that special something that sets you apart… revise your product so you'll have a decided advantage. Without it, you're just one of many players. There's nothing that would immediately stand out to prospects and give you a clear, decided advantage in the market.

What Doesn't Work And Why

1) Weak Openings

Headlines that lack energy and zeal rank poorly on the performance scale. Those that read like a plain-Jane statement, lack the power to attract an audience. This kind of headline produces a ho-hum reaction, at best. And if that's all your headline does, you don't stand much of a chance.

Following is an example of a typical, weak headline. I found this on a direct mail letter that was personally addressed to me. The surprising thing about this sample is the name associated to it. Coming from such a prestigious institution -- and a business school at that -- I would have expected much better. In fact, I can hardly imagine a poorer headline choice that this one.

> *"ABC* University's Marketing Program: Creating Competitive Advantage November 16 to 21, 1997... ABC's School Of Business ABC University, Anytown, Ontario"*

* the actual name and specific location of the institution have been changed. The rest of the headline remains exactly as published.

I bet you're thinking to yourself... *"Wow! What a zinger!"* Would this make you reach for your checkbook to sign up immediately? Well... you can probably figure out how successful they were in filling this class with such an impotent headline.

In effect, weak, boring statements tell prospects *"This messages is rather ordinary. You may read it if you like, but there's no new information -- no great secret -- revealed here. Your time is better spent elsewhere."*

2) Creating Confusion By Attempting To Be Clever

Any headline that cannot stand alone and be self-explanatory to each and every prospect in an instant, is not a strong headline and should not be used as the tool to attract audiences.

Take a look at the following example:

"If it got business done any faster, we'd have to install airbags!"

Huh? What's your first reaction to reading this headline? If your response is anything resembling mine, than you'll see why this collection of words is a poor choice for a headline. This headline by itself is completely unclear. Granted, it did have a visual with it... but that's beside the point. Headlines have to stand on their own. They have to be able to do the job solo, otherwise, there's no reason for it being there.

The writer of the above example tried to be cute. But instead, they only created confusion – a definite no-no. You've only got one brief, fading moment for your headline to use all it's power to catch the eye of your prospect. Don't waste your most valuable moment by trying to be cute, clever, or humorous.

3) Company Names And Logos As Headlines

This is one of the most common advertising mistakes in general—certainly the biggest blunder made by Yellow Pages advertisers. That's not the only place you'll find ridiculous ad-openings like *"Al's Roofing"* or *"Peter's Pet Food"*. Just flip through any daily or community newspaper. It won't take you long before you discover an advertiser who hasn't yet figured it out and continues to use his company at the top of an ad where a real headline belongs.

As I'm writing this, I reached for my copy of the local Yellow Pages. I randomly selected a page and landed upon the category of *"Lift Trucks"*. On this particular page there are 10 different display ads that all fit under this category. These are the large ads that cost advertisers considerable money every month. Just take a look at the "headlines" I discovered.

Here they are:

Fork Lift School And Truck Driver Training
Alco Equipment Inc.
All-Lift Ltd.
BT Canada
Topline Equipment Co. Ltd.
Canada Material Handling Ltd.
D&K Forklift Service
Carrier Lift Truck Service Inc.
J.H. Ryder Machinery Limited
J.H. Thomas Industries Ltd.

All but the first one (and this is certainly no "killer" headline by any means) feature a company name and/or graphic in place of a compelling, benefit-oriented headline. Looks like a case of "follow the follower". If just one of these companies took a different approach and focused their ad around a strong headline, their message would capture a lot more attention, they'd reach prospects sooner and they would likely be the beneficiary of additional business as a result of their Yellow Pages advertising.

Using your company name as a headline is a virtual death sentence for your advertising. What possible appeal could a company name have? The only exception is when the name conveys a benefit of some kind like *"Instant Plumbing Repairs"*. Chains that have huge brand recognition like *McDonald's*, are another exception. Prospects actively seek out those names. But for the large majority of businesses, this kind of marketing is just plain dumb.

Most names wouldn't qualify as representative of any kind of benefit. These names should never be used as headlines -- ever. Let your competitors advertise this way if they want. But don't be tempted to follow their lead, even if they appear to be successful and you only want the same results. Success is usually the culmination of a multitude of factors, of which advertising is only one. Don't make the mistake of believing their success is due to their advertising brilliance.

Sure, this other company may be doing plenty of things right. But I can assure you that if they're using a name as a headline... they can't possibly be getting the best return on their advertising investment. Any benefit-oriented headline would almost certainly provide a better return.

4) Vague, General Descriptions That Could Easily Be Tied To Other Products

When developing the single, most important component of any type of communication -- the headline -- it's crucial to focus on what separates you from the crowd with a unique message that's exclusively yours. It's crucial that you emphasize the uniqueness of your product, service, or offer and do so in a way that means added benefits and value to your prospects.

A vague, general description is the exact opposite of a specific, hard-hitting, original presentation of a unique benefit.

Here's an example:

"24-Hour Plumbing Service At ABC Plumbing."

What's wrong with this headline? Well…let me ask you… what's unique about the message here? The way I see it… there's nothing particularly special about the ABC headline. 24-hour service is something most people would expect from a provider of household plumbing services. It's something that any competitor could also offer, if they didn't already. There's nothing unique here. No special appeal.

I would suggest a different approach. Here's a quick rewrite:

"Plumbing Problems? -- Have An Expert Plumber At Your Door Within 33 Minutes Of Your Call, 24 Hours/ 7 Days A Week -- GUARANTEED!"

Making the same claim as a competitor gives you no upside leverage. There's nothing special to it. It possesses no additional zip… no firepower. It lacks impact because it offers no clear-cut advantage over others.

These kinds of claims simply blend in with the rest of the pack and therefore, are incapable of producing the desired result of maximum response. If what you promise is the same as what others promise, your headline will surely underachieve. You can easily add sales appeal by revising your headline to present what you do in the way that means the most to your prospects.

6 Simple Rules For Writing Captivating Headlines

Here's a handful of tips to keep in mind whenever you need to develop a dynamite headline:

1. **Target your ideal reader.** Identify the prospect you want to attract within the copy of your headline.

2. **Your first mission is to get this ideal prospect's attention.** That's the number one priority. If you fail to capture attention, your message won't be heard.

3. **Use benefits that appeal to the self-interest of your prospects.** Create a headline that suggests to prospects that you have something for them that they genuinely want.

4. **Be bold and daring.** Always stay on target by making any claim or attention-getting statement relate to your product, service or message.

5. **Make your headline easy to read and understand.** Instant impact is what it's all about. Hit hard and hit fast with something that's sure to lure the interest of your prospect.

6. **Concentrate your efforts on capturing attention and sparking interest.** You must interest prospects, but... you can only do that after first gaining their attention.

The Attraction of The Specific

Specifics sell. Therefore, if you want to sell more, communicate in real, measurable terms. Actual numbers tell a true story and make it easier for your audience to understand, appreciate and relate to the power of your statement. It's an instant credibility booster, particularly in testimonial-style headlines, although it can have a significant impact on all other types as well. Actual numbers. Real amounts. It conveys a more realistic and attainable result because it doesn't appear to be something that's been "made up" to suit a marketers wishes.

Compare these two examples for impact:

Example #1: "Protect your money from devastating market corrections."

Example #2: "Here's A Time-Tested, 100%-Guaranteed Way To Average A 23.78% Return On Your Money --Every Year-- No Matter What Happens On The World's Stock Markets!"

It's possible that both headlines above could be used to market the same training course. But which one has more power? Obvious, isn't it?

The first example mentions a benefit. If you've ever lost money in the markets, protecting your money in the future is probably one of your major investment concerns. But if all you wanted to do was protect your capital, you probably wouldn't be in the market in the first place. Chances are you also want the best return possible. But, what would that be? The second headline presents a specific amount -- something that anyone can easily comprehend and recognize as an outstanding promise. It also offers a strong, specific guarantee -- *"a time-tested, 100%-guaranteed way"*-- to achieve the big payoff.

Try removing those specific references from our sample.

You'd be left with something like this:

"Here's A Way To Make More Money Every Year, No Matter What Happens In The Stock Market!"

On the upside, you're still left with a benefit statement. But without those specific numbers, the headline's power is noticeably diminished.

Keep in mind that you've got to be able to back up any numbers you use in your headlines or body copy. Insist upon accuracy. Use test results, trials, and actual client testimonials to gather data you can use to add the power of specific references.

Talk To Your Prospect -- One On One

One-on-one communication works because it gets through to the prospect. It addresses the reader as an individual, something that appeals to the ego and captures the attention of audiences of all kinds.

Perhaps the strongest word you can ever use in a headline is the word "you". *You* addresses the reader specifically, and immediately catches the reader's eye as something of personal significance. It's a targeted communication that speaks directly to prospects.

When you communicate one on one about something your market is interested in, you build instant rapport as your prospect senses your empathy. One-on-one communication creates a special bond between messenger and recipient, resulting in a more receptive and enthusiastic response. Of course, it takes an accurate understanding of exactly what it is your market needs and wants. If you miss the mark with something that simply doesn't appeal, no amount of personal communication techniques will have much of an effect.

Here are three examples of headlines that communicate, one-on-

one:

> "Are YOU Paying TOO MUCH For Auto Insurance? Look Inside To Discover How To Save Hundreds Of Dollars."

> "We'd Like To Help You Take Advantage Of The Lowest Interest Rates In Decades. That's Why We've Pre-Approved YOU For A $10,000 Scotia-Line Personal Line Of Credit."

> "SPECIAL PREFERRED CUSTOMER OFFER INSIDE! Dr. Napoleon Hill, The World's Greatest Authority On Success, Has Never-Before-Released Video Message For You! PLUS -- A FREE Stereo Cassette Player Worth $29.95!"

Don't Present The Product-- Present The Reasons Why Prospects Should Be Interested

Products and services don't sell themselves. As you now know, it's the benefits -- real or implied -- which build interest and induce more prospects to buy. You only have mere seconds to attract interest. Don't waste precious time by talking about your product or service. Instead, shout out what is most likely to draw them in; a huge benefit.

Benefits are what we all want. It's the reason we buy products and services. It's why we willingly exchange our hard-earned money for products and services. Attractive benefits make it easy to spend our time and money because the perceived payoff far out-weighs the dollar or time costs.

Benefits help prospects move closer to their goals, large or small. Benefits are the solutions and helpful advantages that make prospects say, *"Wow! What a great idea! I need one of these, NOW!"*

Remember… it's not the products or services themselves that interest prospects and turns them into active buyers. It's what that product or service does or promises. Those perceived advantages makes it appealing and that's essentially what buyers are buying.

Here's a headline that announces a new product:

"Introducing, the Excalibur 360 Lawn Mower From Green Lawn Machines."

Where's the benefit in the headline above? Don't search too long… you'll only drive yourself crazy. There simply isn't one. Now there is an element of news here, but… there's no benefit offered. It's simply an introduction of a new machine. The prospect is left to guess for himself what the actual benefit is.

Always stress the benefit to your audience and always prioritize according to what benefit has the greatest appeal to your specific market.

Here's another headline -- but this one stresses the benefit, instead of merely introducing the product:

"Introducing… Easy Does It Router Secrets! Now You Can Easily Make Those Tough Cuts With The Simple Secrets Of The Pros Revealed In This Exclusive Video."

Your Primary Objective Is To Convince The Prospect To Read On

Headlines "sell" the reader on reading more of your content or copy. The headline is your introduction to the rest of the piece, so it's got to work very hard at convincing readers to stay because it's in their best interest to do so.

Plant a seed of possibility. Immediately capture the imagination and focus of your audience by interestingly or provocatively suggesting an appealing payoff.

The individual who happens upon your headline is looking for reasons to avoid reading the details and spending any more time with your message. He's trying to eliminate the clutter from his crowded life and will only pay attention to those messages that seem to speak directly to him about those things that are near and dear to his heart.

Those are the very messages that captivate and compel because they're on the same wavelength as the reader's own thoughts. These ideas resonate with the reader and instantly establish a priority ranking -- making them worthy of at least further investigation by the prospects.

Headlines that win, get through to the prospect as something that's worth their time and attention because of the subject matter. You've got something for him... something extremely interesting... something that's worth acting on to get or at least to learn more about. It's something specifically directed at the prospect; a solution to a problem... a way to achieve an improved result... or, a step closer to a dream.

Make It Believable

No headline -- however grand its claim, or big its benefit package -- will ever achieve the desired result without being believable. That's why specific results -- the actual facts and figures obtained by others or through actual testing, is so valuable.

Scrutinize your own headline creations for believability before testing. If your claim appears to be "too good to be true" -- your audience won't believe you and your efforts will fail. Many people are naturally skeptical, and it's this skepticism that you must try to overcome if you want to make the biggest impact.

Job #1: Capture Attention

First and foremost, the headlines you write should be composed with the idea of capturing attention and winning an audience. You want to reach out to a special group of people; your prospects. Those are the only folks who matter, in terms of your communication.

So how do you go about attracting the attention of your best prospects?

Method #1: Use keywords that cut right to the heart of your prospect and get him to raise an eyebrow at your offering because of its perceived importance, timeliness or relevance. You'll find a list of several great headline words and phrases to use, later in this manual. Choose your words with care. Mix proven performers with words of specific significance to your prospect.

Method #2: Present the major benefit in the first few words -- the ideal end result your prospect really wants on an emotional level. Make your benefit so obvious that your prospects cannot ignore it.

Method #3: Present an appealing offer that's difficult or impossible to resist. Make it so alluring, inspiring, and attractive that your audience can't resist finding out more because to do otherwise is to miss out on the offer of the year.

Whenever you can, place your headline in a large typeface to give it greater prominence on the page. Big, bold letters portray a degree of importance and consequently attract the eye first. By really making your headline stand out visually, you have a better chance to gain a readership. But if your words fail to captivate and inspire continued reading, you'll quickly lose the interest of those you briefly attracted.

2 Important Keys To Success: The Venue and the Appeal

As important as headlines are in terms of the overall success of your advertisement or marketing piece, you cannot overlook the importance of placement.

Where will your headline be running? Is it reaching your best, most qualified audience? Consider the venue and project both a *best* and *worst* case scenario in terms of response.

Are you reaching a large enough audience, or should you be using alternates to target greater numbers?

I raise this issue simply as a reminder to keep the end goal in mind at all times. The best headline ever conceived will not give you the results you're looking for if enough of your prospects never see it. Obvious perhaps, but an important point to keep in mind nonetheless.

In considering your options, strive for the maximum number who fit your profile as prospects for your offering. Circulation numbers are usually of little importance. Your market usually represents just a portion, large or small, of a publication's total circulation.

Don't fall into the trap of thinking every one who buys it or receives it, is a true prospect. Rarely is this the case.

Get The Reader To Mentally Experience The Enjoyment Of All The Benefits

The more effectively you can transfer the experience of "benefit ownership" to your prospect, the more effective you'll be in drawing him in and converting the sale.

Benefits are what matter most. Yes, I know… I've mentioned this before. But, I cannot stress this point enough. Benefits sell. When you can get your prospect to take ownership of the benefit in his imagination and get him to *see* and *feel* the full value of the benefit, you've gone a long way to gaining his undivided attention and interest. And you've lessened his resistance to buying your product.

Benefits feed the desire within the heart of your prospect. You want to figuratively transport your prospect to a magical place where all his wants, dreams, and desires can be instantly fulfilled with one wave of your magic wand. Use powerful, evocative words -- words that conjure up images and ignite the wonders of the imagination.

Offer Useful Information In The Copy Below

What makes prospects read beyond the headline? Well, apart from satisfying curiosity, prospects are drawn in by the promise of the headline: *the promise of a payoff that can be their own.* It's this reward for reading -- *what the prospect perceives he'll get out of it* -- that justifies the extra effort and time required to read further.

Give prospects information. Tell them what they'll get and show them how to do it better. Share insider secrets that will enhance their use of the product or service even further. Provide tips, helpful advice, or reveal some valuable, usable information.

Often you can attract a larger audience by offering to reveal a taste of what your product provides in the headline. Make sure your copy reveals whatever you promise. If you offer a free report, you'd be well-advised to deliver a report in addition to your sales material, rather than disguised sales material only. It's okay to place your report within the content of your sales material. Just be sure to deliver on whatever it is you promise or you'll only disappoint prospects in the long run.

What's The Big Idea?

It takes a big idea to capture attention and get people to read your message. How do you know when you have a "big idea"?

1) *It will fit in perfectly with your market and the chosen medium.*
2) *It will be totally unique in your market.*
3) *It will most likely be revealed in one of those "Aha!" moments.*

Create the most alluring offer – the largest promise -- that you possibly can. Turn your product, service, or message into something that promises to provide the reader with a tremendous advantage of some kind. Make your product the answer to your prospects dreams. What dream can you help to fulfill?

As you develop various headline possibilities, always strive to make your benefits and your offer even more inviting, more compelling, more interesting. Ask yourself this question constantly, *"How can I make it bigger, better, more attractive, or more appealing?"* Work at evolving your *big idea* into one with massive promise and built-in irresistibility.

Idea Starters

Think about the factors that are important to your prospect. Then hint at a secret -- that special something about your raw materials, ingredients, processes, sources, or methods that would most impress your target audience.

Recall anecdotes from your personal or business history. Use this human interest information to create an original headline that intrigues and captivates. Forge a connection with your past that casts you in a new light -- one that's potentially advantageous to prospects.

Empathize with your target market. Begin from the mindset of a typical prospect. Get inside his mind. Communicate from a solid understanding of your prospects thoughts and feelings of the moment. Empathy removes the barriers and shortens the distance between you and your prospect.

Empathy builds rapport. Your ability to come from an understanding of your readers point of view, gives you an advantage and makes you a likely candidate for the prospect's attention, interest, and business.

Observe the headline techniques of major consumer magazines and supermarket tabloids. Many such publications rely on newsstand sales, so the appeal of the front covers and more specifically, those featured headlines, are of paramount importance. Notice how these headlines are created to motivate the reader to read on.

Challenge assumptions. Break from tradition. Non-conformity can lead to breakthrough headline concepts. Be open to creative ideas and be willing to push the envelope and test new approaches.

Choose descriptions that emphasize the unique value of your offering and that lend legitimacy to your company, product, or service. Indispensability and credibility are two powerful qualities for attracting huge interest.

Explore your personal bookshelf, filing cabinet, and the local library for headline ideas. Seek out various information sources that relate to your business. Magazines, books, manuals and newspaper clippings can all provide fertile ground for headline ideas. Pay particular attention to article headlines, subheads, book titles and chapter titles. Look for trigger words, thoughts, concepts and observations that can jump-start your creativity and build on these idea boosters.

Look to unrelated fields for headline ideas. Recast these headlines to suit your own application. This method will help you develop a headline message that's completely different from your competitors. Customize the idea to fit your specific target market.

Brainstorm words and phrases related to your product or service. Think of both features and benefits. Just let your mind flow, unrestricted by limitation. Write down every idea, even those seemingly ridiculous or outrageous thoughts. At this stage, you simply want to generate a steady flow of ideas. Think and write. Do not edit. Afterwards, review your list and expand on those possibilities with promising appeal. (for more on brainstorming, see the chapter on headline formulas)

Learn from proven successes. Take what works elsewhere and apply it in a way that's compelling, memorable and persuasive. Review direct mail samples that arrive in your mailbox, particularly, those you've received more than once. Successful mailers are very direct in their delivery. Most profitable mailings get right to the point with benefit-oriented headline copy, presented with clarity and unveiled promptly.

Chapter 6

69 Tips For More Effective Headlines

1. **Grab your target prospect by the jugular!** Get right to it-- don't beat around the bush. Reach out daringly and directly in a way that's impossible for prospects to overlook.

2. **Make your headline tempting, teasing, and tantalizing.** Touch a nerve in your prospect. Generate a headline that's difficult to forget so your prospect is "driven" to find out more.

3. **Keep it clear and concise.** Refine… rewrite… reduce… and otherwise modify until you have your headline down to a brief statement with an unmistakable message. Craft a handful of words that resonate with your prospect. Most people today prefer information in quick, easy to digest, bite-size pieces.

4. **Compose your headline with an understanding of the sheer volume of competing messages that are all vying for the same prospect's attention.** You want people to perk-up… to pay attention to your message… so you need to develop a headline that advertising-weary eyes will find appealing. Entice prospects into the rest of your message with a riveting opener.

5. **Consider it your most important hook -- a line or two you run at the top of a display ad or marketing piece to lure attention.** In effect, your targeted headline says this, "Here's something important, unique and of value to you, dear prospect. Pay attention here or you'll miss out".

6. **Stick to a single, coherent idea or concept with your headline.** Focus on one powerful thought that is easily understood and absorbed in an instant. Think of your headline as a "grabber" that must be compelling enough to interrupt the busy prospect and get him to notice your message. Your headline does its job when the otherwise indifferent reader is pulled into the body of your message. One strong idea is all you can reasonably expect busy people to grasp in a quick glance.

7. **Summarize your main selling point as a headline.** Readers should get the gist of what your entire message is about by reading headlines and sub-headings only. By offering your strongest selling point up-front, you help attract prospects who are genuinely interested and you'll help turn away the "tire-kickers".

8. **Capture attention quickly.** The single, most important task of any headline is to get noticed. One way to get noticed is to stand out from the crowd. Think of your ad as a telegraphic communication, conceived for the purpose of attracting qualified attention from the maximum number of prospects. Your headline needs to hit hard and hit fast.

9. **Be careful about making statements that others could easily claim as their own.** Generic benefits that others offer are too common to be effective. Add an original twist with a specific promise or result. Do something radically different and you'll get noticed.

10. **Convert facts into meaningful prospect benefits.** Avoid headlines that are mere factual statements about a product or service. The facts are only features and features by themselves, don't sell. Prospects are attracted by what those facts mean. It's the sizzling benefits and mouthwatering descriptions that draw huge numbers of prospects.

11. **Be upbeat and positive.** Paint a bright future. Offer workable solutions that provide hope and inspiration to your audience. Avoid gloomy, negative headlines. Raise the spirits of your audience with an upbeat, helpful approach.

12. **Simplify your message so it's easy to grasp.** Don't force people to stop and think about what it is you're trying to say, or you'll quickly lose the audience. Your prospects won't waste any valuable time trying to figure it out. Make it easy for them.

13. **Distinguish your message from all others.** Take a road less traveled. Try an approach that's different from the typical or traditional. You'll attract more attention when you break the mold and do something that sets you apart.

14. **Strive for a provocative headline.** Formulate words that jar your prospect to grab his attention. Be interruptive and benefit-oriented. Compel your audience to read on to get the full story. Insist on the strongest, most compelling collection of words. If your headline fails to capture an audience, the rest of your message won't even be noticed. Be bold. Pull out all the stops to seize maximum attention.

15. **Distill your most unique advantages or benefits down to one powerful sentence that packs a punch.** One format that works is to string your top three benefits together into one statement. Choose the most important, most valuable claim or promise you can offer your prospects. The appeal of a huge promise is what lures prospects.

16. **Choose the best 6 or 7 headlines from your longer list of possibilities.** Then, put yourself in your prospect's shoes and select the one heading most likely to stop you in your tracks, if you were scanning a page of classified ads or flipping through a magazine.

17. **Do the unexpected.** You'll arouse interest and curiosity so the reader will be drawn in to find out more. Catch prospects by surprise with something interesting. Anything out of the ordinary quickly commands attention. The worst thing you can possibly do is to offer the same old boring headlines that have a similar look to many others.

18. **Zero in on the thoughts that are foremost on your prospect's mind.** The more accurately you pinpoint this mindset, the more likely you'll engage the interest of an increased number of readers. Research is the key.

19. **Spark interest by first identifying a problem the prospect has been forced to endure because until now, there was no alternative solution available.** Identifying the specific problem helps target qualified prospects, builds rapport, and then sets up the scenario for your new, improved miraculous or magical solution.

20. **Craft a headline that piques the reader's interest.** A good headline makes you want to know more. It induces interest by planting a seed of possibility.

21. **Customize a famous quotation so it supports your sales message or enhances a major benefit.** Look for quotations everywhere and save them in a file folder. When you need a headline with a different twist, pull out your file and begin playing around with different word combinations.

22. **Indicate why your audience should believe your claim.** Provide detailed proof later in your body copy, but at least hint up-front, at some credibility-building evidence to justify your claims. A sub-heading is a great location to suggest supporting proof.

23. **Trigger a powerful emotion in your audience.** Add a "feel good" or "peace of mind" component and your message will be well received. Present benefits that evoke powerful emotions. Determine what the important issues are that influence prospects, and then zero in on these key concerns. Headlines that stir emotions motivate active readership.

24. **Try presenting what your product isn't, before revealing what it is.** This helps to carve out a special niche in the marketplace and it arouses curiosity because the reader can identify with claims about what your product is not -- which is exactly the thing many competitors are pushing.

25. **Appeal to the anger and frustration experienced by prospects.** This tells the prospect that you're acutely aware of the problem and you understand how he feels. Bingo! Instant rapport.

26. **Be clear enough in your wording to at least hint at the benefit you have to offer.** If the main headline isn't crystal clear on the benefit offered, use a sub-heading that directly expounds on that benefit. Avoid blind headlines that may attract attention, but aren't followed up with a big benefit promise.

27. **Turn passive, scanning readers into active, interested prospects by encouraging action by issuing a direct command somewhere in your headline.** Many people, consciously or unconsciously, prefer to be lead by others, rather than initiating an action. Including a call to action can help boost response.

28. **Establish a position of prominence by raising the perception of your product or service to heroic status.** Make a compelling

promise. Elevate your new, alternative solution to a superior level. Use this strategy when offering a radical, new approach to a long-endured problem that's costly or challenging to deal with. Anything that makes life easier, more enjoyable or less expensive… a solution that promises more gain and/or less pain, could be considered a welcome addition to the marketplace.

29. **Ask a question.** Provoke people to ponder. Relevant, targeted question headlines are something few can resist. They involve the reader and draw him deep into the heart of the message. Carefully constructed question headlines beg to be answered and therefore, pull prospects inside.

30. **Encourage prospects to take action.** Challenge the reader to make things happen… to take charge… in order to improve some condition or circumstance in their lives. Use an alluring promise with a substantial reward.

31. **Deliver a clear, complete and understandable message within your headline.** People generally read headlines as a complete unit, taking in all the words as a single image, instantaneously. That's why it's so important to achieve clarity. You don't want to create a mixed meaning or leave anything open to interpretation. A clear, complete message helps you reach more prospects, including those who normally read headlines only. You want genuine prospects to quickly recognize the importance and relevance of your message.

32. **Pique curiosity with short, punchy headlines that get your prospect thinking and wondering.** Your goal is to at least get people to find out more. To do this effectively, you must quickly deliver the payoff. Any curiosity angle used, must be directly related to the product or a benefit. Headlines that arouse curiosity without an obvious connection, rarely succeed. Instead, these teaser headlines are a quick turn-off for real prospects.

33. **Give your prospects something to think about.** Create an interruption. A pause for thought involves their mental faculties. Get them to question an established method or belief, or to re-think a decision. Raise an issue and pull them in.

34. **Surprise prospects by announcing that your new benefit-laden solution to their problem is actually derived from a simple or**

unusual source. This technique increases their interest and involvement with it's surprising revelation.

35. **Act fast.** Quickly serve up the most alluring advantage you can offer, since that's all most readers see. Grab your prospect with opening words that persuade him to spend more time with your message because of the huge gain that it promises.

36. **Pre-test your headline before using it by soliciting immediate feedback from others.** Choose carefully those whose opinions you seek and closely monitor their first impressions. It's those initial, instantaneous reactions -- without allowing time to stop and think about it-- that most accurately reflects the response a typical prospect may have.

37. **Present the purest rationale for using your product or service.** Deliver a simple, straightforward statement of what they'll get and why it's a better choice for them.

38. **Dangle free premiums, gifts, bonuses, or other enticements that add extra value to the benefits of your product.** Any free offer may help marginally, but the best results occur with a direct connection to that which is being offered.

39. **Add a news angle to your product or service that would make it more interesting to your market as a whole.** Make an announcement that has a newsworthy feel to it.

40. **Speak the voice of your prospect.** Communicate what a genuine prospect might actually be thinking or feeling and you'll create instant interest as readers relate to your thoughts. This kind of headline acknowledges and empathizes with the prospect, by expressing a valid concern, in the prospect's own voice.

41. **Capture and "frame" a shortened segment of your customers actual words of appreciation.** Solid third-party endorsement headlines lend credibility to any presentation. Since buyers were once prospects themselves, the views of other people in similar situations often carry extra weight with first-time buyers.

42. **Write your headline as though you're creating a billboard.** You probably have only a few seconds to get your main selling point

across. Work at distilling your most powerful and provocative sales argument down to something which can be quickly and easily understood. Give the skimming reader the opportunity to get your essential message in one quick take. Jolt them a little, to get them to pay attention. Think of your headline as a visual siren, one that zaps attention briefly.

43. **Review your collection of customer testimonials.** Keep an eye out for any key statement that could be used in whole or in part, as a unique headline. Look for those comments that ideally reflect what you want other prospects to know about your product or service. What is it your prospects want? Pick out a few good testimonials and choose the best 3 to 12 word description that provides the essence of a great, attention-grabbing opening line.

44. **Play around with various headline possibilities to evolve the most effective headline.** Often the best headlines are unexpected and therefore have stop-ability built-in. An unexpected headline presented with visual impact while instantly delivering a clear, important benefit or payoff, is a surefire winner.

45. **Deliver a straightforward claim about how the prospect will gain by having or using your product or service**. Here's an example: *"Cleaner dishes without the effort"*. Now take that declaration and embellish it for added impact. *"Cleaner dishes automatically in 58% less time -- guaranteed or your money back!"*

46. **Tell a story.** Infuse your message with your own personal twist. Many best-selling books are emotional stories about people. Capitalize on this widespread interest by hooking prospects with an intriguing lead-in. Storytelling headlines attract attention due to their human interest qualities.

47. **Offer a reward in your headline -- a reward for reading the rest of your message.** Promise a payoff and then deliver on your promise. *"10 ways to save hundreds of dollars on your taxes."*

48. **Think like a journalist.** Answer the who, what, why, where, when, and how. Combine two or more of the most interesting or most relevant answers into one short statement. To see how this is done, simply review your daily newspaper and take note of the

headlines that capture your attention.

49. **Invent the perfect solution to your prospect's problem, as though you possess magical powers.** Identify the *dream solution* -- that one big benefit any prospect would ideally want to gain from your product or service. Present that perfect solution in your headline and... deliver on the promise. Be sure to adjust the product, or the headline copy to achieve compatibility.

50. **Combine "how to" with your biggest benefit.** The headline that begins with *how to* offers a practical solution and delivers a specific *want*. "How to" is a certain headline winner in many situations and it's an easy formula to use. Simply insert your benefit after the words "how to".

51. **Define your greatest strength or advantage in a single word or phrase.** Then take a pencil and a pad of paper and sketch out how that single advantage might look in visual form. Nothing fancy here, just a quick, rough sketch. Then, describe the scene you've just created in the most alluring, prospect-centered language and shape those words into a headline with appeal.

52. **Uncover a distinction -- pinpoint a specific advantage or accomplishment that would impress your prospect.** Then play around with a few different ways to communicate this fact. Do it right and you'll momentarily mesmerize your audience.

53. **Consider using lead-ins to headlines.** Lead-ins are short opening statements that help set up or introduce a main headline. Lead-ins are most often used in large display ads and sales letters. Another use for lead-ins is to identify the target audience.

54. **Compliment your main headline with a subhead.** Subheads can be one or two lines of sales copy that offer a payoff, or additional support to the main headline. Subheads add believability and help reinforce your major message.

55. **Combine the power of a lead-in, main headline and sub-heading to present a more complete message including multiple benefits and a compelling offer.** The various components must work together to deliver the gist of your message quickly.

56. **Edit your headline so it passes the "quick-view" test.** Pare it down as much as possible. Typically, prospects scan headlines in just a few seconds and then move on to something else unless the headline has caught their interest or piqued their curiosity. The faster you can deliver something of interest to your audience, the better.

57. **Handle a long headline two ways:** 1) break it up into a major headline and subhead or lead-in, or… 2) emphasize one or more key words in extra large type so those big, bold words deliver a sufficiently strong message on their own. For option #2, seek out the services of a skilled graphic designer.

58. **Tweak your headline until it's a real "stopper" for those you hope to reach.** In all forms of communication, the first thing a prospect sees, reads, or hears, has a significant effect on the overall results of the entire message. First impressions are crucial in gaining an attentive, interested audience.

59. **Capitalize on the use of readily available tools to help with headline creation.** Your handy reference section might include a dictionary, thesaurus, encyclopedia, books of famous quotations, trivia games and books, as well as the *Guinness Book Of World Records*. These resources provide valuable kindling to help you evolve an eye-stopping headline.

60. **Write a headline that would make you sit up and take notice.** Ask yourself, *"If I were the prospect, would this headline appeal to me and pique my interest?"*

61. **Address your audience directly, in a style most appropriate to the subject matter.** Fine collectibles suggest a style of elegance and grace, while an appeal to business people would be more successful with a straightforward, factual presentation with an emphasis on the return on investment.

62. **Select your opening words with great care.** The first few words of your headline are the most important. Capture attention and interest as quickly as possible. Compose an evocative handful of words that touch a nerve.

63. **Test headlines whenever the opportunity arises.** Sometimes a

slight adjustment, or a completely different approach altogether, can have a dramatic effect on the results.

64. **Tuck away your chosen headline for at least 24 hours, or longer whenever possible.** Go back and look at your headline with fresh eyes and a less biased opinion. If your headline still retains a powerful punch, you've probably developed a winner.

65. **Make it more attractive to your prospect to stop and discover your complete message, rather than move on to something else.** Use your headline to persuade prospects to read the rest of your ad by suggesting that the copy beyond the headline contains useful and valuable information.

66. **Lure prospects with just enough information to get them interested.** Whet their appetites. Hook them first with a tempting promise before offering up the rest of your message.

67. **Project credibility and believability.** Make certain that any claim is not only 100% true, but that it also appears to be true in the eyes of your prospect.

68. **Write all headlines in the present tense to more easily get the prospect to put himself or herself in the picture.** By placing your benefit promise in the present tense, it seems much more real and attainable to the prospect.

69. **Provide the "reasons why" when offering an exceptional deal.** Give prospects an accurate explanation for special discounts offered in your headline. Sharing the real reason adds believability and makes any outstanding offer appear much more legitimate.

Chapter 7

7 Simple Headline Formulas

The very first thing you should do is take the time to decipher every possible benefit of your product, service or article. Yes, it's recurring theme because it's that important. Uncovering benenfits is essential preliminary work for any of the any headline format you choose. The reason is clear: *benefits generate interest and sales.* So if you haven't yet taken the time to uncover the benefits, now would be a good time to do so. Without this kind of list in front of you, your task will be much more difficult.

The easiest way to begin compiling a list of benefits is to start with the features. Features are easier to come up with than benefits. All you have to do is examine your product, service or company, and write down all the attributes that describe whatever it is you have to offer. List everything you can think of pertaining to your product or service. Then, convert each feature into a benefit. (Review the section on benefits in Chapter 1)

Typical product features include:

materials used in the manufacturing process
materials used for packaging or self-storage
ingredients
packaging components including storage cases, product
dispensing, freshness, seals, etc.
colors
sizes
functions
speeds
extra accessories
options
finishes
component parts and the function of each
efficiency
assembly
instructions

warranty/ guarantee
flexibility of use
durability

For a service, features might include:

hours of operation
shopping choices – shop at home, in-store showroom,, drive-through, web site
delivery
installation
warranty/ guarantee
accessibility: phone, fax, email, store-front or office location
maintenance
planning
consultations
frequency reminder service

For a business, a list of features might include:

customer service
business philosophy
mission
warranty/ guarantee
hours of operation
shopping choices

Once you have a list of the features that come to mind… take each individual feature and express it in terms that make it meaningful to your prospect or customer. Turn each feature into something prospects and customers would really want – *a breakthrough benefit*. Add sizzle. With each feature, ask yourself, *"What does this mean to my customers and prospects?"* Capture all the ways others are greater advantaged by owning rather than not owning.

Formula #1: The Ultimate Benefit – FAST & EASY!

When you've taken the time to list all the benefits of your product or service, it's much easier to begin formulating some excellent headlines.

Decide on the most attractive benefit your product offers. What one great advantage does your product give customers? What unique advantage does your product offer? Don't just guess at it -- talk to prospects and customers. Give them a short list of 2 to 5 solid benefits your product delivers on and then ask them to choose just one – the one that means the most to them.

What you hope to achieve with this little exercise, is to get your actual market to identify the one benefit that is of supreme importance to them. It could be a single benefit or, more likely, the *ultimate benefit* of your product. Try to narrow it down to one powerful benefit or advantage and then use that as your starting point.

A headline that's centered around the most appealing benefit has a good chance of attracting far more interest and attention than any non-benefit headline.

Step #1: Identify Your BIG Benefit

Step #2: Provide A Quick & Easy Way For Prospects To Experience The BIG Benefit

"Quick and easy" satisfies the craving for instant gratification with little or no work. What could be better than that? Not only are you promising the one thing customers want most, but… you're also offering this in rapid time and without much, if any effort on the part of the prospect. This is how you present the ideal *dream solution* to your customers and prospects. But you have to make sure your promise is believable.

Specific solutions attainable in less time and with less effort -- that's what people want. Your job is to give it to them up-front in the headline. One way to do it is to simply add the words *quick and easy*. Another technique is to quote specific figures in terms of the time required, such as *"10 days to…"*, *"30-day plan for…"*, *"…in just six weeks"* or *"overnight"*.

<u>**Examples**</u>

"Discover 7 Quick & Easy Ways To Writing Super-Responsive Classified Ads"

"I'll Teach You How To Quickly & Easily Get All The Credit You've Ever Wanted -- 100% Guaranteed -- Or I'll Pay You $50 For Wasting Your Time!"

"Discover The Simple, Yet Little-Known Secrets For Creating Your Own Best-Selling Information Product In A Single Evening!"

"In Just 27 Minutes, While Sitting In Your Most Comfortable Chair, You'll Discover Everything You Need to Know To Create Your Own Dynamite Web Site That Brings In Cash Daily"

"In Less Than 30 Days, You'll Notice A Huge Improvement In Your Vocabulary Using Our Simple Pocket Guide For Only 5 Minutes A Day. It's A Fast And Easy Way To Make A Huge Difference In Your Life"

"How To Give Yourself The Gift Of Daily Inspiration Quickly, Easily – Even Automatically"

Formula #2: The "Borrow It" Approach

This technique borrows ideas, words, phrases, and formats from other headlines and adjusts these to suit. It takes individual components from existing headlines and repackages them to suit your product, service, or offer. Here, you choose different headlines that you like and combine features of several to create a hybrid.

This technique works for both simple and complex headlines. You simply string together a few parts that appear to be a good fit and then substitute your benefit or offer to suit.

Never copy someone else's headline word for word. That's theft. But no one can take exclusive ownership of any word or phrase. You're always free to use any word or description in your own unique way.

It's an easy way to put together a solid headline in just minutes. The key is to find lots of headlines that you like and to have them ready -- right in front of you. You'll find plenty of examples within this manual package, but you should remain on the lookout for others too.

You never know when you'll want to adapt a phrase or technique for a headline of your own. With your own file of collected headlines, commonly referred to as a "swipe file", you'll have a virtual resource center of adaptable ideas and techniques.

Following are some examples of simple adaptations from original headlines:

Original: "They Laughed When I Sat Down At The Piano But When I Started To Play!~" (John Caples)

Adaptation:

"They Laughed When I Sat Down At The Piano. They Stopped When I Picked It Up." (Gold's Gym)

Original: Breakfast Of Champions! (Wheaties cereal)

Adaptation:

Breakfast of Millionaires. (Barron's financial magazine)

Original: "What Four-Letter Word Do You Use When You Have To Write A Check For Your High Healthcare Premium?" (Jerry Fisher)

Adaptation:

"What Four-Letter Word Do You Use After Stepping On The Bathroom Scale?"

Original: "To People Who Want To Write -- But Can't Get Started"

Adaptation:

"To People Who Want To Own A Beautiful House -- But Can't Get Started With A Regular Savings Plan"

Original: "10 Ways To Lose Extra Weight and Keep It Off!"

119

Adaptation:

"3 Ways To Rid You Home Of Pests and Keep Them Away For Good!"

You can take virtually any effective headline and adapt it to your own product or service. Try different options and arrangements. Insert a new word or phrase. Test it out. You'll see how easy it is to develop a powerful headline by using parts of others to piece together one that fits your purposes well.

You can add a new and interesting twist to this formula by substituting a few words with powerful, provocative, eye-catching replacements. (Refer to Chapter 9 for specific examples) Sometimes just one word can make a substantial difference in readership and results.

Formula #3: The Brainstorm Technique

The brainstorming technique is an excellent way to generate innovative, breakthrough headlines. This technique can be performed as a group exercise, or individually. Both applications can work well to produce original ideas and concepts that can lead to awesome headlines.

The idea of brainstorming is to completely free the minds of all participants and to simply let the ideas flow -- unrestricted and unencumbered -- without limitations of any kind. This free-wheeling, creative activity lets you generate an infinite amount of possibilities.

The best way to brainstorm a headline is to think in terms of customer benefits and stick to short descriptions of one to five words. Open up your mind and let the creativity flow. Try to think of single words and phrases that describe the benefits of your product or service.

It's a liberating experience, one that can often provide a fresh new horizon from which to base your promotional efforts upon.

There are 4 simple rules to follow for maximum results in brainstorming:

1. Place a time limit of 5 to 10 minutes on the actual idea

generation stage. This is the first step where raw ideas are produced and captured on paper, digital recording device, or a whiteboard.

2. All answers should be encouraged. No idea is a bad idea at this stage. Every contribution, no matter how outrageous or ridiculous, should be welcomed and recorded. Do not edit. Keep the ideas flowing. Spit out as many as possible.

3. Stop on schedule. Don't try to prolong a creative session. 5 minutes is plenty of time to gather lots of good ideas to explore.

4. Now, you can start to edit out some answers that don't appear to be on the mark. Take what's left and work with those to formulate a powerful headline.

Example #1

Product: Apples -- Sold By Mail Order

Brainstorming Results:

Fresh, Delicious, Succulent, Vibrant Red, Fresh-Picked, Healthy, All-Natural, Crunchy, Nature's Finest Food, Pure Health, Pure Energy, From God's Garden, Nature's Gift, Give Yourself A Lift, Bite Me, Ummmmm, Wow!, Organically Grown, Individually-Wrapped, Wholesome, Too Good To Be True, Country Crisp, Nature's Finest Gift, From Nature's Bountiful Basket, Fresh To You, Fresh-Picked, Shipped Same Day For Peak Freshness, Rare, Hard To Find, Shipped By Mail, Hand-picked, Tree-Ripened, Exclusive To Okanagan Valley, Sun-Ripened.

Possible Headlines:

"Fresh, Delicious, Organically-Grown, Sun-Ripened Apples Like You've Never Tasted Before -- Delivered Right To Your Door!"

"Give Your Family A Healthy And Delicious Treat From Nature's Best Garden."

"Indulge Yourself With A FREE Sample Package Of One Of Nature's Most Wholesome, Delicious And Nutritious Foods."

Example #2

Service: Gift Selection And Shopping Service

Brainstorming Results:

Choose The Perfect Gift, Show Your Thoughtfulness, Imagine Their Reaction, Make It Right, Wow! I Love It!, Very Impressive, Stunning, Immaculate, Elegant, Enchanting, Awesome, Considerate, Caring, Exquisite Tasteful, Choose Right, Save Time, Forget The Hassles, Hate Shopping?, They'll Love It—Guaranteed!, Impress Them, Perfect Gift Solutions, Gifts On Target, On Time, On Budget, Helpful Solutions For Busy People, Your Shopping Partner, Hassle-Free, Reap The Rewards, Show You Care, Personalized Service, Prompt Delivery, Beautifully Wrapped, Find It, Ideal Gifts, Delivered With Class, Shower Someone With... (Love, Care, Attention) Guaranteed To Be Well-Received.

Possible Headlines:

"Show Them How Much You Care With A Custom-Selected Gift From Magic Moments. We Find It, Pick It Up, Wrap It And Deliver It. You Get The Credit."

"Show Your Exquisite Taste, With An Original Gift They'll Never Forget."

"Impress Them With The Perfect Gift That Shows Your Thoughtfulness, Originality And Exquisite Taste."

"Here's An Easy Way To Find The Perfect Gift, Show Your Appreciation And Demonstrate Your Exceptional Taste -- Without Leaving Your Office! 100% Satisfaction Guaranteed!"

Example #3

Product: Portable Water Filter

Brainstorming Results:

Is Your Water Safe? Kill All Contaminants, Kills Germs, Wipes Out

Harmful Pollutants, Enjoy Fresh Water, Double-Filtered, Safe, Healthy, Fresh, Pure, Purify, Sterilize, Filter, Portable, Adaptable To Any Faucet, Quick Connection, Travelers Companion, Works Anywhere, Fits In Any Suitcase, Compact, Convenient, Taste The Difference, Delicious, Safe Water, Double The Protection, Filters Invisible Contaminants, Take It Anywhere, Guaranteed Safe, Quality, Built To Exacting Standards, American Made, Replaceable Parts, UV Sterilizer, Rugged, Lightweight Steel Construction, Saves Big Money, Eliminates Costly Bottled Water, Snaps Into Place Instantly, Ideal For -- Cottage Owners, Boaters, Travelers, Works Anywhere, Filters 57 Known Contaminants.

Possible Headlines:

> Travelers! Now You Can Enjoy Fresh, Safe, Delicious Drinking Water -- Wherever You Go! New Compact Device Filters And Sterilizes Too For Maximum Purification!

> Attention Travelers: Beware Of Unsafe Drinking Water! Here's Your 100% -- Guaranteed Safe Water Solution That's Easy To Carry, Instantly Connects To Any Tap and Gives You Fresh Filtered Water Wherever You Are -- Anywhere In The World!

> 100% -- Guaranteed Safe Water For Travelers, Cottagers And Boaters! New, Lightweight & Compact Mini-Magic Quickly Connects To Any Tap To Instantly Filter AND Sterilize -- Giving You Safe, Healthy Drinking Water Wherever You Go!

Formula #4: The Power-Packed Combination

Here's a technique that adds extra power to any single-benefit headline. It can be used in several different ways, all with the multiplied power of several components working hand in hand. A combination headline could include multiple benefits, a benefit plus an offer, even a benefit, offer and a guarantee. With the "Combination" headline, your options are plentiful. But the one you select should be the one that packs the biggest punch and works well in your particular vehicle of communication.

The benefit combination approach simply stacks one major benefit onto another in a sequence that usually consists of *three separate benefits*. The result is a headline with three times the power of a single benefit.

The easiest way to begin generating a power-packed combination headline is to begin with a single benefit statement.

Here's one we can start with:

"*Learn To Make Money Like A Millionaire*!"

This headline promises a benefit, but could it be made stronger using the combination approach? Before deciding, play around with several different options.

Let's try out a few possibilities:

"Learn To Make Money Like A Millionaire... Invest Like A Wall Street Wizard With Average Returns Of 37%, Or More... and Create A Future Of Style, Comfort and Unlimited Financial Security!"

"Learn To Make Money Like A Millionaire! Attend This FREE 2-Hour Seminar And Discover The 13 Key Principles Of Self-Made Riches Guaranteed To Make YOU More Money Than Ever Before! Only 75 Seats Available -- Reserve Yours Today!"

"Start Your Own Business, Take Complete Control Of Your Future and Learn How To Make Money Like A Millionaire -- Starting Today."

See how easy it is? The possibilities truly are endless. But obviously, the angle you take is dependent upon your product the market you're trying to reach, and the venue you're using to communicate your message.

Following are some other combination headlines taken from my collection of ads, sales letters, direct mail packages, brochures and assorted other marketing pieces.

This sample delivers a benefit and offer combination:

"Free Video Reveals 11-New Ways To Make Huge Amounts Of Cash... Even During A Recession!"

In this example, a question is used to first involve the prospect. Next, it's immediately followed-up by an offer and a benefit.

"Do You Have What It Takes To Succeed At Your Own Business? This Free Book Will Help You Find Out. YOURS FREE! Starting Your Own Business... 12 Steps To Success."

Here's a quadruple-benefit headline. Watch how much more impact it has vs. any single benefit alone.

"Maximum Profit Direct Marketing! How To Win Tons Of New Customers, Get Them To Buy More Often, Increase The Dollar Amount Of Every Sale, And Double Your Profits In Record Time!"

This headline includes a benefit, guarantee and special offer.

"Now You Can Easily Double Your Profits By Learning The Jealously-Guarded Marketing Secrets Of The Richest Service Companies In The Country... And I Guarantee Results! Plus... If You Act Now, You'll Also Get Valuable Free Bonuses Worth Over $975!" (Joe Hammer)

Using the combination technique is an easy way to boost the appeal of any headline. Start by listing a handful of benefits. If you have a strong guarantee and a compelling offer, include those as well. Then, experiment with different combinations. Vary the order. Try a new angle and soon you'll have the headline you're looking for.

Formula #5: Forget Your Product -- Deliver The Dream

What do your prospects want most? You already know the answer. It's always the benefits that they seek. They want an advantage or a better way of doing things. Solutions to problems and new alternatives that save time, money, and effort. And there's no better option for prospects than the one that does it all. This product is the solution to their dreams.

The idea of this headline technique is to transform your product into an ideal answer to your prospects deepest desires and aspirations.

In order to supply the dream solution, you have to know what your prospects want... their likes and dislikes... their frustrations and disappointments with other apparent solutions. What is it that annoys prospects most regarding your type of product, service, or industry?

Armed with this valuable knowledge, it's easy to see what it would take to provide a better alternative. But you don't want to simply settle for being better than the other choices available. You want to be the ultimate solution to your prospect's problem. What would your prospect really like to have, to be, or to accomplish, that his present choices don't provide? What is the perfect solution -- the best case end result?

So... now it's time to play the role of the wizard. Put on your cape, reach for your wand and create a *magical* solution. Pretend that you have almost God-like powers and that you can give your audience the *ultimate solution* -- that really big benefit or inside advantage they really want.

Your job is to bridge the gap between where your prospects are now and where they would ideally like to be.

Imagine the perfect end result. Create the vision of the underlying desire your prospects hold within. Then, present your message as the ultimate answer -- the optimum solution. Next, set out to fulfill that desire with your miracle product.

Examples:

In the following example, the writer obviously knew his audience well. Most people who attempt new diets, have tried others before without much success. Talk to anyone who has been on a diet and they'll often tell you that afterwards, they gained more weight than they previously had lost. Yet the search goes on for the perfect diet -- one that delivers results without taking away one of life's greatest pleasures. How could any dieter resist?

Here's how copywriter, Jerry Fisher created a dream solution:

"Lose 30 Pounds In 30 Days On Strawberry Shortcake!"

In the next example, Ted Nicholas demonstrates his thorough understanding of the prospects he wanted to target. Anyone who has ever given a speech, has the goal of delivering a stellar performance. What better way to feel the accomplishment than with a standing ovation?

> "How To Get Enthusiastic Response -- Even A Standing Ovation -- Every Time You Speak!"

Next, marketer Gordon Alexander knew something about his audience before he conceived the headline below. I'm sure you've heard the line, *"Give a man a fish, you feed him for a day... but, teach him how to fish, and you feed him for life."* Learning how to make extra money one time, is appealing to many opportunity seekers. But learning how to do it as often as they'd like has much more appeal.

> "12 Weeks To Freedom. Make $5,000 Within The Next 3 Months -- and Never Look Back. Learn How You Can Earn $5,000 In The Next 12 Weeks, and Then Make $1,000 or $2,000 or Even $3,000 Or More -- IN CASH -- Every Week For The Rest Of Your Life!"

Be a dream provider and your headline will attract more qualified and interested prospects and your sales will skyrocket as a result.

Formula #6: Use Your Customer's Own Words

The actual words of satisfied customers holds a lot of weight with prospects in virtually all markets. The words of others -- people who once were in the same situation themselves -- have greater power to influence a prospect's decision than the words of the advertiser.

Gather any feedback that you may have already collected from customers. Review all the letters, faxes, words of appreciation and general comments you've heard in the past. Survey past customers for additional feedback, or solicit a review by a well-respected authority in your field. The more material you have to draw from, the better and more explosive your headlines will likely be.

If you don't have such a collection, now would be a good time to start one. Record words, phrases, reviews and comments and attach the attributed real name of the actual person who made the statement. Jot these comments down and keep a print copy. Request permission to use their words in your marketing material. Most customers are happy to help out this way and appreciate being consulted first.

Using testimonials gives your message a different perspective; one that prospects can more easily relate to. A strong testimonial headline speaks to the prospect in a language he understands, about something he truly desires.

Examples:

Let's start with an actual excerpt I received from a customer who had just received my booklet on writing successful classified ads.

"One of, if not the best investments I have ever made! This information is not only timely and informative, but it actually works. I learned more from your advertising book than all of those $39.99 to $200.00 courses you see on TV!"

Some additional examples:

"WalkFit Is The Best Thing That Ever Happened To Me!"

"I lost 33 Pounds In 30 Days With This Simple Plan. I Have More Energy And I Look And Feel Better Than I Have In Years. Thank You Miracle Diet!"

"I've Tried Every Other Cleaner On The Store Shelf. Nothing Even Comes Close To The Shine I Get With SuperClean!"

Another form of endorsement headline you could try, is an indirect testimonial headline. It works best in cases when there's a "voice of authority" speaking the words and therefor *suggesting* an endorsement.

"Police Say Buy It" (Jerry Fisher)

"8 out of 10 Dentists Surveyed Actually Recommend EasyChew Gum For Cleaner, Whiter Teeth."

"All-Night Donuts -- Rated Number One For Taste By Those Who Ought To Know: Police Officers and Tow-Truck Operators"

Formula #7: Fill In The Blanks

This formula is amazingly easy to use. Just take any or all of the samples provided and adapt them for your own use. Simply fill in the blanks with the appropriate description, expression, action word, or benefit. Once you get the hang of it, you'll want to refer to this section again and again. Not only is it easy, it's also a lot of fun.

Don't feel limited by these suggestions. You could literally adapt any headline found anywhere, and do the same thing. Just transfer your benefits, offers, guarantees, etc., to any headline that grabs your attention. This is a great way to generate a dynamite headline in a matter of minutes. Any one of these fill-in-the-blank formulas could help you create a winning headline for your product or service.

We'll start with the easiest first. All formats assume that you've clearly identified the major benefits of your product. If you don't know what the big benefits are, you'll have a tough time, even with these templates. Several examples are provided immediately following each headline format.

1) **How To...**

How To _____ (get, have, acquire, own, profit from, etc.)
_____ (the biggest benefit your product delivers)

"How To Solve All Your Money Problems Forever!"

"How To Make $87,000 Per Year As A Magazine Writer!"

"How To Easily Get All The Credit You Could Ever Want!"

"How To Increase Your Profits In Any Economic Climate!"

2) **Secrets Of...**

The Secrets Of _____ (the ultimate benefit your product delivers)

"The Secrets Of Living In Style Without Any Money Worries!"

"The Success Secrets Of The Most Prolific Magazine Writer In America!"

"The Secret To Getting All The Credit You Ever Wanted -- Even If You've Been Bankrupt!"

"The Secrets Of Not Just Surviving, But Thriving In Today's Tough Economic Times!"

With your *Ultimate Benefit* you can plug in several other possible formats as well. Fill in the blank spaces below with your biggest benefit.

The Complete Program For _____

The Complete Guide To _____

The Quick And Easy Way To _____

_____ For Fun And Profit.

The next format can be adapted to suit any application you have in mind. Not all components are absolutely necessary. For example, you may have only 2 benefits, instead of 3, as used in this example. Or, perhaps the time factor doesn't really apply, or the guarantee doesn't fit. Adapt it as you like to suit you and the application.

3) Stacked Benefits...

How To Get _____ (Benefit #1), _____ (Benefit #2), and _____ (Benefit #3)... In Just _____ (actual time period such as the number of hours, days or weeks required) Guaranteed, Or (your money back, double your money back, it's free, etc.)

"How To Get A Gorgeous Tan, Relax In Complete Comfort and Be Safely Protected From Harmful UV Rays While Gaining That Natural, Golden Look All Over... In Just 6 Weeks -- Guaranteed -- Or You Pay Nothing!"

"How To Grow Your Business, Gain More Free Time And Profit Like Never Before After Just 3 Easy Sessions -- Guaranteed!"

"Look Here For More Than 150 Time-Saving Ideas That Will Help You And Your Staff Get Organized, Accomplish More In Less Time, With Less Effort And Resistance -- Guaranteed Or Your Money Back!"

4) Problem/ Solution…

No More _____ (major pain or anxiety). Here's A _____ (quick & easy, remarkably simple, little-known, etc.) Way To _____ (achieve the ultimate benefit)

"No More Bad Hair Days! Here's A Proven Way To Maintain The Perfect Look Any Day Of The Week!"

"No More Wet Beds! An Amazing Technique From Europe For Training Your Child In Just One Week. Try It Risk-Free -- 98.7% Success Rate!"

"No More Nervousness! No More Fear! Learn The Tricks Pros Use To Speak With Ease To Any Size Of Audience."

"No More Lost Sales! Here's An Automatic System For Timely Follow-Ups With Every Prospect."

5) How To… Guaranteed…

How To _____ (get the ultimate benefit) Quickly & Easily—100% Guaranteed!

This format can also be used with an implied "how to".

"How To Comfortably Write Your Own Book Or Screenplay In 2 Weeks Or Less -- 100% Guaranteed!"

"How To Save An Extra 20% On Every Book You Order --
Automatically -- 100% Guaranteed!"

"Master The Skill Of Video Editing This Weekend. Discover The
Inside Secrets Of Doing Professional Work With Ease -- In Just
Minutes. Satisfaction Guaranteed!"

6) Get Benefit Fast, Regardless…

_____ (Have, Get, Be, Enjoy, etc.) _____
(benefit) In _____ (time period) Guaranteed, No Matter What
_____ (your age, condition, bank account, skill level, etc.)

"Get Fit In Record Time -- Guaranteed, No Matter How Out Of
Shape YOU Are!"

"Enjoy Gourmet Meals Any Day Of The Week -- Regardless Of
Your Kitchen Skills!"

"Speak Fluent French In 28 Days --100% Guaranteed -- Even If
You've Never Taken A Single Foreign Language Class In Your
Entire Life!

7) Solve A Problem…

(Beat, Overcome, Laugh at, Master, etc.)_____ (major
problem or anxiety) With This Little-Known _____
(secret, solution, remedy, cure, etc.) from _____ (some
unusually simple, or mysteriously exotic place)

"Wipe Out Depression For Good With This Little-Known Natural
Remedy Found Deep In Forests Of The Amazon!

"Eliminate Your Money Worries Forever With The Simple 3-Step
Formula Developed By A Formerly Desperate and Chronically-
Evicted Housewife."

"Overcome Any Fear Almost Instantly With This New 2-Minute

Technique Revealed By A World Famous Speaker."

8) **Visualize It…**

Imagine… (You A) _____ (proud possessor of the "dream" Example – famous artist, millionaire entrepreneur, skilled, in-demand computer technician)

> "Imagine… You A Millionaire Real Estate Investor!"

> "Imagine… You On Top Of The Best-Seller List!"

> "Picture This… You Open Your Mail Box and Find It Stuffed With Literally Hundreds of Cash Orders! Welcome To The Exciting and Profitable World of Mail Order Marketing!"

> "Imagine… Sipping Pina-Coladas On The Sun-Drenched Beaches Of Beautiful Antigua Where There's Always A Gentle Breeze In The Air And The Most Difficult Decision You Face All Day Is Which 5-Star Restaurant You'll Choose For Dinner Tonight."

9) **Number Of Ways To…**

_____ (specific number) Ways To _____
(dramatize the big benefit— "Permanently Wipe-Out Creepy Household Pests, Take The Bite Out Of The Coming Tax Increase, Knock The Socks Off Inflation, Make More Money From Home With Your Own Internet Business, etc.)

> "7 Easy Ways To Save Money On Groceries Without Clipping Coupons And Running All Over Town Just For Those Sale Items!"

> "13 Secrets -- Inside Information Car Dealers Hope You Never Discover About Getting The Best Bargain On Your Next Car!"

> "101 Little-Known Ways To Add Massive Perceived Value To Your Home So It Sells Within Days For At Least 99.5% Of The Full Asking Price!"

10) Reasons Why...

_____ (number of) Reasons Why You Should _____
(major warning or stacked benefit)

"9 Reasons Why You Should Immediately Be Concerned About
The Quality Of The Water Flowing Through Your Taps."

"47 Reasons Why It Not Only Saves You Money To Use Our
Advertising Services, But It Actually Puts More Cash In Your
Pocket -- 100% Guaranteed!"

"There Are 3 Very Good Reasons Why Some Direct Mailing
Succeeds... and You Already Know 2 Of Them. The Third Reason
May Be The Final Piece Of The Puzzle That Makes Your Next
Mailing Click."

11) Problem Solver...

_____ (State the prospect's problem as a
question) Here's A _____ (proven, time-tested, 100% safe,
guaranteed) Way To _____ _____ (get the ultimate
benefit)

"Stressed Out Every Month By Nagging Bills? Here's a 100% --
Guaranteed Way To Live A Worry-Free Life And Enjoy All Those
Things You Thought You Never Could Afford!"

"Worried About Your Child's Grades In School? Here's A
Guaranteed System For Turning C's Into A's, Improving
Concentration, And Transforming Your Child's Own Self Esteem!"

"Losing Money On The Stock Market? Earn 29% On Your Money
Every Year!"

"Finding It Impossible To Keep Off Those Extra Pounds? Now
You Can Stay In Great Shape And Still Enjoy All Those Foods
YOU Really Love!"

12) If… than…

If You're _____ (describe the prospect want)
We Offer _____ (Benefit #1) _____ (Benefit
#2) _____ (Benefit #3)… Plus… (Bonus Benefit)

"If You're Tired Of Your Old Sofa And Thinking Of A Change, We
Offer A Superb Selection, Helpful Design Consultants And A
Comfortable Shopping Experience -- At The Guaranteed Best
Possible Price!"

"If Your Car's A Wreck And You're Thinking About Another Used
Vehicle, This Free Report Will Show You A Guaranteed Way To
Get The Best Price And How To Avoid Getting Stuck With A
Lemon!"

"If You're Looking For One Convenient Source For All Your
Business Needs, We Offer a Huge Selection of Office Supplies, a
Fully-Equipped Print Shop – Even A Postal Outlet Right on The
Premises PLUS, Ridiculously Low Prices Every Day – All Year!"

Chapter 8

Extra Enhancements That Turn Any Headline Into a Turbo-Charged, Attention-Getter That Pulls In More Prospects and Customers

Add *Quick & Easy* To Your *Magical Solution*

Most of us are looking for simple solutions -- those that take the least amount of resources. Whenever you can, add *quick and easy* to your promised benefit and you'll have a headline with a stronger appeal.

There's nothing like a quick-fix. It's an uncomplicated solution. Instant gratification makes any promised benefit even more enticing. If your solution helps people achieve the desired result in less time and with greater ease... by all means, say so. Anything that makes the necessary action less of a chore, or easier to handle, is welcome news to your prospects.

The "quick and easy" combination helps get prospects off the fence of indecision and moves them towards the action you want; to read further, to inquire, or to purchase your product or service immediately. It removes the obstacle of requiring effort and energy... something many people these days seem to have in only limited supply. Your "instant" solution is often the catalyst to action. It's often the final thing that sways them in your favor. It's that extra appeal that makes your headline seem like a "can't lose" proposition.

You can choose the words to describe your quick-fix from many different options. Here are a few variations to kick-start your creative juices:

- Fast And Simple...
- Idiot-Proof...
- Ridiculously Easy and Fast...
- The Lazy Man's Way To...

- It's So Easy, Even A 10-Year Old Can Do It...
- The 7-Minute Workout...
- In Just 10 Days...
- Just 5 Minutes, Every Other Day, Is All It Takes...
- Instant, Automatic Results...

Here are several examples that begin with a simple benefit-oriented headline, and a revised edition that includes the "quick and easy" enhancement:

Original: "Learn How To Make Money Like A Millionaire!"

Revised: *"In Just One, Power-Packed, 3-Hour Session, You'll Learn 37 Easy Ways To Make Money Like A Millionaire!"*

Original: "We Can Free The Writer In You."

Revised: *"The Quick And Easy Way To Free The Writer Within And Create Your Own Money-Making Books, Reports, And Manuals!"*

Original: "Delicious & Nutritious 10-Minute Recipes For People On the Go."

Revised: *"Introducing... 99 Fast, Easy, And Delicious Dinners -- Created For Busy People Just Like You -- Who Want Wholesome, Nutritious Meals In 10 Minutes Or Less!"*

Combine A Strong Benefit With An Irresistible Offer

An irresistible offer added to a strongly-desired prospect benefit is a potent combination that works to pull more readers in than any single benefit statement alone ever could. The key is to combine the two forces of your biggest benefit with your most enticing offer.

The addition of an offer to a benefit headline, gives it that much more pulling power. The benefit answers the prospects question -- *"What's in it for me?"* and the offer gives the prospect that little extra push needed to get him into action.

Offers are designed to stimulate action. The best offers are limited in some way. This has the effect of creating urgency in the mind of the prospect. Prospects know that they better act now, or risk losing out on your offer altogether.

Your limited offer may be time or quantity related. The best offers usually promise something of value -- free. *"Free for 15 days…"* clearly states the time limitation. *"Only 75 seats available -- book yours now"* expresses the limited availability of a product, in this case, admission to a public seminar.

Following are some examples of benefit/offer headlines:

"Master The Art & Science Of Writing Killer Ads And Sales Letters! Call Before August 1st For Your Free Audio CD"

"How To Set And Achieve Goals Right On Schedule, Every Time. Your First 3 Lessons Are Absolutely Free Without Obligation. Discover The Step-By-Step Plan To Achieving Anything You Really Want -- FREE!"

"Whole Foods -- Not Pills -- Will Help You Look Better, Feel Better, Be Happier And Live Longer! Here's Your FREE Guide To The Best, Life-Giving Natural Foods On Earth."

Convey Your Unique Advantages Over Other Available Options

Whatever it is that most advantageously distinguishes you from all competitors, that's what you want to bring out in your headline. It's this key idea that you want to make very clear in the beginning.

Your individual edge is what helps set you apart from the crowd in dramatic fashion. It's your own original twist. You need a unique approach with your headline, something that's as different from the run of the mill messages as night is to day.

Your job is to find the one angle that's unique and then capitalize on it. Find that thing your product does better than others. Or, stress a benefit that others have failed to seize as their own. Another approach is to add an uncommon variation to the way your industry traditionally markets its products. This will ensure that your headline is very different from any others who may be vying for the same prospects.

"Why Settle For A Typical Cleaning Service That Only Spreads The Dust Around When You Could Have Your Entire Home *Vacuum-Dusted* For Cleaner, Healthier Living?"

"At ABC's, Our Selection and Value Are Unmatched. If You Can't Find The Exact Name-Brand Item You're Looking For, We'll Pay You $10 On The Spot, Plus... We'll Rush Order It From Our Supplier And Deliver It To Your Door." and... We'll Match Any Price, Anywhere -- Guaranteed!

"Professional Quality Workmanship and Guaranteed On-Time Project Completion, Plus... We Thoroughly Clean The Entire Work Site At The End Of Each Day To Make Your Renovation As Painless As Possible!"

Add Original Character And Flair To Your Headline

Be original. Add a unique element to your headline that will clearly and decisively distinguish your message from every other. Make yours stand out by giving it a new twist that adds impact and intrigue. People are tired of the same old vague, generic, commonplace messages that lack originality and interest-arousing power.

Find something that's clearly different about you, your product, offer, guarantee, or business. Then, play up that distinguishing quality for all it's worth! Use any angle that can make you seem more credible, your offer more reasonable, or, your message more interesting or intriguing.

Here are some examples:

"The Amazing Direct Mail Secret Of A Desperate Nerd From Ohio!" (Gary Halbert)

"Starting Off With $56,000 In Debts... A Young Divorced Mother Tells How She Became A Millionaire In Only 34 Months."

"Kansas "Tornado Chaser" Captures Amazing Footage Of Survivors Weathering Mammoth Twister That Carves A Mile-Wide Path Of Unbelievable Destruction!"

"Prize-Winning California Tomato Farmer Says Growing Grapefruit-Sized, Juicy Beefsteak Tomatoes Is Easy When You Take These 3 Simple Steps."

Replace Unnecessary Words

Once you've selected a headline to test from your (hopefully long) list of possibilities, you should review each and every word. This is very easy to do with such a small number of words to review.

Of each word, ask the magical question: *"Does this word add to the power or comprehension of the headline?"* If the answer is "no", eliminate the offending word -- it has no place in your most important sentence. Any unnecessary word should be eliminated at once. Any word that's lacking in descriptive power, clarity, and most importantly, *impact* -- should be replaced with something that can do the job more effectively.

Here's a sample of a published headline taken from my collection of direct mail pieces:

"Begin training now for an exciting career in Desktop Publishing and Design. The ABC Certificate Program can be completed in half the time, and costs less than half the price of our full Diploma program. Once you graduate, you'll be able to continue the full program, and take delivery of your computer immediately!"

Total: 53 Words

Here's a quick revision designed to eliminate words that don't really contribute anything:

Become skilled in Desktop Publishing and Design in half the time and at half the cost of the full Diploma program. Complete the Quick-Start Course and take delivery of your new computer immediately as you continue working towards your own diploma.

Total: 42 Words

Still, this "headline" should be pruned some more. But I wanted you to see how quickly you can edit and revise headlines to eliminate excessive words. The more you refine your work, the easier it becomes and the more effective you are in producing pithy, hard-hitting headlines.

Multiply The Value Of The Offer

The stronger the offer, the more prospects you'll move into action. If your offer is truly appealing, it deserves a place in your headline. Providing a compelling offer means you're casting a wider net and you'll increase your pool of interested prospects by default. Offers can include a special introductory price, a product sample or trial version, bonus items and discounts with a deadline.

Here are 3 secrets to turn any offer into a surefire winner:

1) Make it so appealing that it's difficult or impossible to resist...
2) Make it exceptionally easy to take advantage of...
3) Make any bonus or premium package valuable enough as a stand alone item to be well worth the action required.

Chapter 9

Magical Words and Phrases For Winning Headlines

What Kind of Words Work Well In Headlines?

The best words to use in headlines are those that:

A) Speak directly to the reader…
B) Appear to be the answer to the reader's prayers…
C) Are easy to read and instantly understand…
D) Involve the reader by allowing him or her to visualize themselves enjoying the promised benefit…

When you speak directly to the reader, you've got his attention. He is the targeted recipient of your message. Hint at the ultimate answer to a problem, or the big benefit desired and your message will be perceived as being worthy of the time and attention required. After all, it's something he really wants to have, be, or do.

If the reader cannot grasp what you're saying with unquestioned comprehension, your headline won't get you anywhere. Simple words that have just one meaning to your prospect are the best words to use. Action words create excitement and draw readers in, carrying them through the rest of your copy. *Action words are vibrant and alive, rather than boring and academic.*

Words and Phrases

The right words help you express the function of your product or service with flair. They add color and drama to your presentation to make it more interesting. Try to use words that evoke emotions and vivid mental pictures. Let your prospect enjoy a little fantasizing about what his or her life could be like.

Employ selected words solely for their shock value. Stop readers in their tracks. You demand attention by using words and phrases not normally associated with your type of business, product, service, or your chosen communications vehicle.

Add an original twist. Do something that's slightly off-kilter. Out of the ordinary words, phrases, questions and combinations are naturally interruptive, capturing the attention and arousing the curiosity of the scanning prospect.

Avoid worn-out, generic descriptions and all clichés. Common expressions that have been used over and over again lack the important headline requirement of stop-ability.

Find words that characterize what you're offering in a descriptive and appealing way.

Incorporate unusual or descriptive company or product names into your headline. But be aware that most typical names probably aren't good candidates for this technique. It takes a special name to make this work. A unique or catchy name linked by association to a powerful benefit can have far-reaching positive implications.

Consider using quick-phrasing combinations that communicate instantaneously, without the need to read each individual word in order to comprehend the meaning. Instant recognition phrases include such combinations as: *free report, 24-hour service, lose weight,* etc. The sooner you can transfer your message to the mind of the over-stimulated, time-poor prospect -- the better.

Add pizzazz by linking your benefit to a well-known name. Using a name that prospects can relate to, increases readership due to its' instant recognition. Possible names include famous people, cities, buildings, tourist attractions, companies or well-known products.

Use words that have attention-getting capability because they aren't often used for promotional purposes. Commonly used terms simply blend in, producing less than desirable results.

Select a small group of words that resonate with your audience. Choose your words wisely. You only have a few short seconds to capture attention and interest. You have only one shot at winning an audience. Develop your most powerful and most concise sales message.

Employ strong action words that involves prospects and activates their interest.

Capture and record attention-getting words culled from other sources such as radio ads, billboards, magazines, etc. Jot them down and later transfer these to a file folder or computer file that you can use as a reference the next time you need to come up with a great headline.

Try stringing together several of these words into a powerful headline. This gives you another formula for creating effective headlines.

Proven Effective Headline Words

You	
You're	**Eye-Catching Words**
Secrets	
Now	Secrets
New	Amazing
Free	Shocking
Proven	Revealing
Money	Surprising
Guaranteed	Magic
Magic	Seductive
Winning	Important
Introducing	Warning
Announcing	Suddenly
Results	Stop
Facts	Urgent
Easy	Vital
Instantly	Confidential
Breakthrough	Explosive
Amazing	Thrilling
Reveals	Electrifying
Yes	Win
Here	Sex
Quick	Startling
Discover	Stunning
Only	Remarkable
How	Beauty
Exciting	Beautiful
Discover	Sizzling
	Vivid

Dynamite
Heart-Wrenching
Dazzling
Mouth-Watering
Delicious
Gift
Fun
Potent
Mind-Blowing
Successful
Hot
Daring
Alluring
Provocative
Make
People
Money
Results
Sale
Better
Discount
Save
Soar
Unlock
Look
Formula
Blockbuster
Revolutionary

Slash
Secure
Protect
Win
Get
Use
Have
Own
Accomplish
Achieve
Garner
Compare
Make
Hurry
Boost
Burst
Enjoy
Imagine
Explode
Grasp
Reach
Attain
Blast
Profit
Benefit From
Profit From

Action Words

Unleash
Earn
Keep
Look
Discover
Find
Reap
Harvest
Uncover
Obtain

Additional Favorites

Powerful
Strong
Health
Unique
Surprise
Odd
Quickly
Limited
Security
Safety
Safely
Special

Superior
Expert
Ultimate
Increase
Surefire
Fascinating
Startling
Miracle
Fortune
Profitable
Wealth
Quick
Remarkable
Unparalleled
Suddenly
Excellent
Tested
Proven
Reliable
Sensational
Improved
Direct
Better
Refundable
Interesting
Challenge
Profits
Profitable
Informative
Revealing
Practical
Bonus
Plus
Gift
Selected
Instructive
Valuable
Sensational
Trusted
Genuine
Important
Critical

Quality
Sturdy
Unsurpassed
Outstanding
Exclusive
Lavishly
Scarce
Useful
Rare
Strange
Valuable
Discount
Reduced
Lowest
Popular
Special
Wanted
Power
Who
Want
Why
Which
Hot
Attractive
Famous
Successful
Professional
People
Unusual
Weird
Highest
This
Profusely
Absolutely
Simplified
Practical
Colorful
Approved
Delivered
Easily
Authentic
Bargain

Unlimited
Surprising
Beautiful
Big
Huge
Mammoth
Enormous
Gigantic
Colossal
Bargain
Complete
Full
Confidential
Greatest
Helpful
Immediately
Largest
Endorsed
Crammed
Latest
Noted
Personalized
Sizable
Terrific
Lifetime
Tremendous
Unconditional
Wonderful
Formula
Alternative
Truth
Flourish
Enterprising
Solution
Incredible
Crucial
Daring
Explosive
Floodgates
Bonanza
Timely
Energy

Energizing
Surging
Wanted

Favorite Headline Word Combinations and Action Phrases

How To…
How Would…
How Much…
Who Else Wants…
Inside Secrets Of…
Do You…
100%-Guaranteed!…
Little-Known Secrets…
Closely-Guarded Secrets…
How Would…
Advice To…
At Last…
Money-Making…
Special Offer…
Limited-Time Offer…
Act Now To Get This…
Money-Saving…
No-Risk…
Zero-Risk…
Must See…
Must Attend…
The Shocking Truth About…
Do YOU…
What You Should Know About…
Complete Details, FREE…
Free Report (Booklet, Book, CD, DVD, etc.) …
Call Now For …
Limited To The First ____ (quantity) To Reply…
Limited-Time Opportunity…

How You Can…
You Get…
You Have…
Facts You…
Profit From
Save Time…
Save Money…
If You're Serious About…
The Truth About…
Free Bonuses…
The Single Most-Important…
Let Me Show You…
Once In a Lifetime…
Learn To…
Make Money…
Secrets Of The Pro's…
Don't Spend Another…
Trade Secrets Of…
Key Secrets To…
Urgent Information…
Surprising New Discovery…
13 New Ways To…
Do You Feel…
Do You Have…
You Can Start With Less
Than…
Starting Off With…
Yours Free…
Discover How To…
The 3 Secrets That Can…
If You Qualify, You Could…
Yes You Can…
Could This Be…
What Would You Do…
Are You…
If You Have…
If You Are…
No More…
When It Comes To…
Here, At Last…
For Preferred Customers
Only…

Take Advantage Of…
Make The Most Of…
Reserve Your…
Act Fast And You'll Also Get…
Are You Ready…
Nothing Else Compares To…
Our Best-Selling…
New Lower Price…
For Busy People…
If You're Worried About…
Top 10 Reasons To…
You're Invited To…
Prepare For…
The Ultimate In…
Makes Life…
Looking For…
The Perfect…
The Quickest Way To…
Individually Designed…
There's Nothing Quite Like…
One-Of A-Kind…
Personalized Service…
Starts Working Instantly…
The Intelligent Way To…
No-Nonsense Advice…
100% Pure…
Designed To…
Built To…
A Breakthrough System For…
A Breakthrough Formula…
It's So Easy, The Only Thing
You Need Is…
Take One Moment…
Time-Tested…
Proven To…
Everything You've Ever
Wanted From…
It Works …
You'll Never Have to Worry
Again…
Simple But Powerful…
A Safe, Easy Way To…

The Safe Way To…
Worry-Free…
Pamper Yourself With…
Everything You Need To…
Isn't It Time…
A Simple Solution To…
Results In Just…
For The Serious…
You'd Never Guess…
Now It's Yours…
Last Chance For…
Last Chance To…
Absolutely Free…
For Less Than…
Get Ready To…
Join (Hundreds, Thousands,
Millions) Of Others Who…
Used By…
Plus… You Get…
Get Ready For…
Take Advantage Of…
Your Chance To…
The Choice Of…
Knocks Your Socks Off…
Information-Packed…
More Powerful Than Ever…
Free Trial Size…
Yours Free If You Act Now…
Here's How…
Now Available…
Treat Yourself…
Thousands Have Been…
Which Of These…
Astounding New _____
Secrets…
7 Reasons To…
Best-Kept Secret…
12 Proven Steps To…
Reveals Powerful Secrets…
Now You Can…
Proven Steps To…
Gives You The Added

Advantage Of…
Are You Still…
Say Goodbye To…
Closely-Guarded Secrets…
Reserve yours now…
A Breakthrough In…
The Choice Of…
In Test After Test…
Surprisingly Simple…
Remarkably Rugged…
As Easy As…
Easy To..
Hassle-Free…
Makes _____ Easier
(Faster, Trouble-Free, More
Convenient, Disappear, etc.)…
_____ Made Easy…
Easier Than Ever…
You'll Wonder Why…
One Call Away…
One Time Only…
_____ Without The
Problems…
Your One-Stop Source For…
Cash In On…
Everything You Need For…
Professional Results With…
Instant Impact…
Helps You…
The Next Best Thing To…
Unlock The Hidden…
Perfect For Any…
Limited Edition…
Never Before Seen…
It's So Simple, Even…
Satisfaction Guaranteed…
At Last…
Advice To…
100%-Guaranteed…
Guaranteed To…
Unconditionally Guaranteed…
Money-Back Guarantee

No Questions Asked
Guarantee…
Zero Risk…
No Risk…
Guarantees You…
Discover The Magic Of…
Get More…
If You're Looking For…
Learn To…
Beyond Your Wildest Dreams
(Fantasies, Expectations, etc.)
…

For Fun And Profit..
Live Like…
Enjoy The Ultimate…
Experience The Thrill…
You've Never Seen…
For That Special…
What Better Way To…
Tired Of The Same Old…
Instant Results…

Words To Avoid

In your headlines, you'll want to be certain that each word contributes to the collective power of the headline. Keep it upbeat and positive. It's okay to remind readers of their pain, but always follow it up with a powerful, positive solution that promises to alleviate their pain and replace it with pleasure.

Keep an eye out for words that have negative connotations. Eliminate dull, uninspiring words that fail to grab prospects attention. Your task is to keep prospects interested and enthused and this can only be done with words that evoke positive feelings.

Review your headline for words that lack power. Carefully scrutinize your words and edit out any word that fails to: A) contribute meaning, or... B) help hold the sentence together.

Avoid common, generalized modifiers like "very" or "extremely". You'll also want to be sure that your headline is unique and that means not using the same words your competition uses. Take a good look at each and every word. That's how masterful headlines are created.

Following is a short list of words you might want to avoid using in your headlines because of the images associated with them. There's no absolute rule against using these, but if you do, be sure that you don't cast a mood that's too negative or gloomy.

Death	Pain
Destruction	Liability
Dead	Bad
Poor	Failure
Fail	Obligation
Sell	Decide
Hard	Cost
Wrong	Loss
Negative	Contract
Disaster	Worry
Difficult	
Deal	

Chapter 10:

Using Design Techniques To Add Extra Impact

Font Sizes, Styles And Colors

A little variation can go a long way towards creating a headline that is more visually appealing. Long headlines with words that all feature the same *look*, creates the effect of a drab, gray tone that runs right across the page. The simple appearance of words can sometimes have a profound effect on the personality and feeling they evoke.

Your choices of fonts, sizes, styles, and colors are however, somewhat limited by the media of your message. A magazine display ad gives you unlimited opportunity for creative expression. A classified ad on the other hand, has few, if any choices.

If there is one basic rule to follow here it's this: *use type variations in small doses only.* A little variation can be attention-grabbing. Too many variations can turn prospects the other way.

Here's a simple example that emphasizes just 2 words:

The Secret of How To
BE TALLER

In the example above, the emphasized words help to select the audience for the message. Only words that are meaningful and help arouse interest should be emphasized. The key is to create a visual stopper that has special appeal to your prospects. Any highlighted words should be capable of instantly communicating a brief message -- one that's impossible to miss.

Despite the fact you may have a full palette of choices at your disposal, that doesn't mean that you should use them. You may want to add color to your headline to make it stand out and this can work well. But using multiple blends and shades can actually create a visual distraction that takes the focus off your chosen words. Stick to a single color -- something dramatic like a bright red can really stand out in a sea of black text.

Wherever possible, use a larger typeface for your main headline. This is the heart of your message -- your best chance to attract the attention of prospects. Larger, bold type can help to draw the eye and give readers a convenient check point, one that helps determine the next action they take.

The actual type size you should use for your headline is dependent upon the the project, the available space and the number of words in the headline. For as small display ad, you might chose a headline font size of 24 points. For a sales letter, perhaps 18 points would do the job effectively when the rest of the page is set in 12 point type. But sizes can vary. I've seen some sales letters with headlines of 36 points and more.

This is 12 Point Type

This is 14 Point Type

This is 18 Point Type

This is 24 Point Type

This is 36 Point Type

Given the opportunity, I also suggest that you make your headline bold. This adds dimension and bulk to the individual letters that help set them apart from all the other text. ***Since the human eye is naturally drawn to darker objects first, setting your headline in a bold type adds to its eye-appeal.*** You want the reader to know the message of your headline is the most important sentence on the page and that he should read it first.

Set your headline apart from the rest of the message. Make it the most visually dominant text component on the page. By adjusting the size, boldness and perhaps using a different color, you help to draw attention to your headline.

What style of type work best for headlines?

There are a select few fonts that I personally prefer and use most often in headlines. These include *Times New Roman*, *Century Schoolbook*, *Helvetica* and *Arial*. I also like to use *Futura Bold* for small display ads with short headlines where it really has to shout in order to be noticed. The first two are serif fonts. This is the preferred choice for long passages of text as it makes the reading easier. The other cited preferences are Sans Serif fonts.

Basically, fonts or typefaces can be divided into 3 distinct groups: Serif, Sans Serif, and Script. Serif fonts are identified by the tiny "feet" or *serifs* that run off of each stoke of a character. Serifs entice the eye to move from character to character in a smooth, unnoticeable transition which make this an ideal style for reading text of any size.

Sans Serif means characters without serifs -- straight, clean lined text. Their style is straightforward and plain. Hence they deliver an uncomplicated and clear message. The clean lines make Sans Serif text ideal for attention-getting headlines.

Script fonts are modeled after hand-writing and the characters appear to be joined to one another. I suggest you use script fonts only on rare occasions when the situation calls for it. In most cases, you'd be well-advised to stick with a Serif or Sans Serif font for your headlines.

This Is A Serif Font
This Is A Sans Serif Font
This Is A Script Font

Here are a few fonts that I prefer to use in headlines:

Times New Roman
Century

Arial
Impact
Franklin Gothic Heavy
Verdana
Tahoma

Choose A Format That's Easy On The Eyes

It's important to choose a font that's easy to read *at-a-glance*. There's nothing particularly outstanding about any of the fonts I tend to use. But they all offer easy readability, clarity, and the capacity to stand out visually as headlines. And that's the key point here: *you want to draw attention to the words and their meaning, not to the appearance of the text.*

Avoid any font that could be difficult to read. Resist the temptation to add your own design flair to your headlines. Unless you're a skilled graphic artist, you may be courting disaster. You want your message to stand out loud and clear. You don't want to call attention to your design skills. The results, however impressive they may appear to you, may not be the most effective in clearly communicating your benefit message.

Fonts to avoid include any script font. *Commercial Script* or *Shelly Allegro* may look great on wedding invitations, but for most marketing applications, these fancy designs should be replaced by simple, straightforward fonts. Stick to the basics, instead.

Sample Script Fonts:

Freestyle Script

Edwardian Script ITC

You should also pass on any font that is decorative in nature. Opt instead for a simple version that won't call attention to itself. This includes any font that wanders from the basic look of a *Times Roman* or *Helvetica* font, as well as any type that is converted into artwork.

Sample Decorative Fonts (avoid using these):

COPPERPLATE GOTHIC BOLD

Andalus

The best designs are clear and simple with adequate spacing. This simplicity allows for effortless reading and no errors in the interpretation.

If you choose to use reverse type *(white lettering on a black background)* for your headline, you're better off to use a Sans-Serif font as your headline. These reproduce on printed documents such as brochures and postcards with better clarity than do Serif fonts.

Using A Graphic Image Along With A Headline

Here's another design tactic you can employ to add impact to your headline; use a photograph to enhance your communication. The secret is to make sure your headline and graphic work well together to present a single coherent message. A graphic that works well with the headline generates a powerful one-two punch that involves the visual senses in the interpretation of the text.

One important point to keep in mind when using graphics is to make both the graphic and the headline large enough so they cannot be missed. In other words, make it impossible to see one without seeing the other.

Example:

156

Graphic used: line art sketch of a huge baby's head with its mouth wide open in wailing mode.

Headline:
"IT'S 3 A.M. AND YOU DON'T KNOW WHAT TO DO."

"Subhead:
Start Parenthood Off Right With A 2-Hour Newborn Care Consultation In Your Home. It Will Make Things Go A Lot Easier." (Jerry Fisher)

Here's another example of the skill Jerry Fisher displays when marrying a headline and graphic.

Graphic used: sketch of a little house complete with a garden, windows and a door… but in the overall shape of a *lemon*!

Headline:
"WILL YOUR NEW HOME BE A LEMON?"

Subhead:
"Probably not. But before you buy, let us check it out."

The best graphic is often a photograph and the best photograph to use is one that helps convey the benefit message or accentuate the prospect's potential dilemma. I've also seen some clever uses of line-art drawings (as above) that were custom-crafted for each particular application. Note that I didn't say "clip art"-- the kind of graphics readily available to anyone who purchases software or buys images online.

The best visuals are those one-of-a-kind pieces that communicate the message of the headline poignantly and brilliantly.

In choosing a graphic to use with your headline, consider it's value in reinforcing your message. Does it help the prospect to better imagine, visualize or dream about the end result? If it does, by all means, use it. If you have any reservation about this, drop the visual altogether, or find a better one to work with. If your visual doesn't help to convey your benefit statement in some way, it simply doesn't belong.

In some cases, it's worthwhile to add a personal portrait-style photo of you to your headline. This idea can work well whenever you want to establish credibility or a more personal tone to you message. It also adds a touch of realism to the proposition as readers can more easily visualize you "speaking" the words of your headline. It's a way to break the ice with your target market so they'll feel more comfortable accepting your ideas or doing business with you.

This concept is often used in sales letters, where the apparent author of the letter is also pictured to the side of the headline. It works equally well with web pages, Yellow Pages advertising, and community-based display ads for local, service-oriented businesses.

Turning Your Headline Into A Graphic

Another way to inject extra impact into your headline is to turn the headline itself into a graphic. I wouldn't suggest anything too elaborate here -- a simple graphic presentation of your most alluring words should do the trick. It can be as simple as reversing the type -- creating a dark-colored background (usually black) with lettering that appears as white. The idea here is to create a headline with more of a visual component, in hopes of attracting a larger readership.

One obvious outlet for using this technique is your web site. However, you need to pay attention to the size of the graphics file you create, in order to keep page-loading times down to a minimum.

With short headlines, you have more options at your disposal. You can manipulate the text by stretching it or adding a shadow effect. But, let me issue a word or warning here; it usually takes the skill of a talented graphic artist to pull this off effectively.

Typefaces are made to exacting dimensional standards for a reason, and that reason is usually related to legibility. When you tinker with the built-in dimensions of a typeface, you're altering its original design and possibly reducing it's clarity and readability. It can be done with striking effect, but more often than not, the adjustment diminishes the actual results.

Keeping Your Message Clear

You want your headline to do the job and that job is always to capture the attention and interest of qualified prospects and get them to stick around. Your headline is your strongest weapon in winning an audience. Therefore, it deserves to be the major focal point of any message.

If you're using a photograph or line art in tandem with a headline, the headline deserves at least the same prominence as the graphic. In any other format where a graphic isn't used, the headline should act as the dominant visual component and be located where its' message cannot be avoided.

Focus your creative efforts on finding a way to express your big idea with crisp, clear copy. Avoid expressing obscure, wandering thoughts in favor of those that can only be interpreted one way. Focus your message. Channel it's direction. Be direct and to-the-point. Eliminate any extra words that aren't absolutely necessary and that make your headline longer and less direct than it need be.

Key Word Emphasis

Here's a tactic you can use to emphasize certain key words of a headline. Select a few words -- those that deserve special emphasis -- and give them added visual power. You can do this by using uppercase, bold, italic, or colored text. Some marketers also increase the size of the highlighted text.

This technique, like many others, depends on the venue in which your headline is to appear. In a small display ad, key word emphasis may be best expressed through uppercase letters. With many magazine classifieds, emphasis is limited to the first word or the first line of text and is most often characterized by uppercase lettering. In a large display ad, postcard, or sales letter, you have a wider selection of tools to work with.

What specific words should be emphasized?

Emphasize those words that have the most impact on readers. It usually comes down to benefits, offers, and audience selection -- the three most important factors in generating interest with your headline.

Another approach I use on occasion, is to emphasize the word "YOU" in headlines. I want to make sure the reader understands who the message is intended for. *You* has the quality of calling out to prospects and gaining their attention quickly.

There's another word I highlight sometimes. It's the word "and". You may find this one a little strange at first. But I use it to stress the value of an offer or to underline the tremendous benefits suggested.

"Discover How To Feel Beautiful, Sexier, Satisfied, **AND** More Fulfilled With These Top Secrets Of Hollywood Stars"

"Little-Known Techniques To Building Unlimited Wealth Online – Amazing New Facts AND Breakthrough Technologies For Taking Complete Control Of Your Financial Future, Right From The Comfort Of Home!"

There's an important rule to remember when using any tool of emphasis. That rule is restrained emphasis. Use it sparingly, or not at all.

Emphasize too many words and you really emphasize nothing.

Overuse is totally ineffective and will actually weaken your headline. To highlight everything is to highlight nothing. Just keep this concept in the back of your mind when you're thinking about any kind of keyword emphasis.

First Letter Visual Enhancements

This tactic is most often used in brochures, newsletters, magazine articles and annual reports. It's a technique for calling attention to a starting point. By enlarging the first letter of the first word, or by changing its' style of type, you create a visual draw. It's something that's different from the rest of the page, thus pulling the eye to this point, first. What better way to get your prospect to tune into your complete headline message than to place it right in front of him? It's like you've provided the road map, and your prospects will naturally follow along.

First letter visual enhancement options include:

- Raised Caps
- Drop Caps
- Different Fonts
- Different Colors

A "Raised Cap" look is created by taking the first letter of a headline or body copy, increasing its size and placing it on the same baseline as the rest of the text. This gives it a "raised" appearance.

Another option is the "Drop Cap". In this case, you take the first letter of a headline or body copy and "drop" it down to extend over several lines of text (usually the total number of lines in the case of a headline).

Unfortuantely, the word processing program I've used here doesn't allow me to show you this visually, so I'll have to convey the idea with words alone. Imagine the enlarged letter "A" above, in a still larger size and extending down for two or three (or more) lines of text.

This means that the other words are spaced over to accommodate the first letter. Rather than the "A" rising above the top line, it drops down over the first 2 lines and then forces the remainder of the text to adjust accordingly around it.

To use a different font effectively, you simply choose something quite different from the rest of the text and increase it's size. Here, a script font (Blackadder ITC) is used to sharply contrast with the standard, Times New Roman text.

This "out of character" appearance of your first letter catches the readers eye with its unique look. It's something that's clearly different from all the other elements on a page or promotional piece. I prefer to use these enhancements mostly in newsletters, brochures and content web pages. These simple graphic enhancements can add a nice touch to a headline when done effectively.

How To Modify Longer Headlines For Maximum Effectiveness

For longer headlines -- those usually associated with sales letters and full-page display ads -- try using super-headings and subheads. Super-headings are those introductory lines that help to set the scene for the major headline to follow through on. Subheadings merely expand on the idea conveyed in the headline.

Starting on the next page, you'll find 2 examples that use extremely long headlines in an effective manner. Note the lead-in provided by the super-headline, the larger, (26 pt) more emphatic presentation of the main headline, The emphasized word "and", as well as the follow-up power of the subhead.

If you'd like to achieve true financial freedom, here's your chance to master the methods experts use to grow your investments and take charge of your future...

Discover How To Substantially Improve Your Investment Success, Eliminate Costly Commissions **And** Take Complete Control Of Your Financial Destiny – Starting Today!

...Introducing a proven, information-packed program that reveals all the closely-guarded investment secrets to creating a fortune! Make more money and build lifelong wealth, with greater ease and more confidence than you ever thought possible!

If you like to call your own shots... If you want to build your own personal fortune, quietly... methodically... systematically... if you want to take advantage of the incredible technology that's right at your fingertips, now... than, please read this entire letter very carefully...

Now this example is quite long and you may prefer to use a shorter opening. But make no mistake about the power of these additional tools to boost the *right* readers interest, involvement, and excitement about the message in front of him.

Super-heads are great introductions that help to select the audience and provide a spark of excitement and anticipation for what is still to come. The main headline is your power statement, loaded with benefits of importance to your readers. The subhead follows along, usually expanding on the benefits already suggested, adding an enticing offer to the mix, or simply underlying the importance of the entire message to the reader.

Starting off with $56,000 in debts…

A Young Divorced Mother Tells How She Became A Millionaire In Only 34 Months.

Here she explains how you can also start earning enough money -easily- working at home, to retire as a millionaire within 5 to 10 years.

Other Presentation Enhancements

There are other devices that you can use to draw attention to your headlines. Frames or text boxes -- known in the direct marketing field as "Johnson Boxes" -- are simple enclosures that surround the headline, effectively framing it. This sets the headline apart from any other text. It's a ttechnique most often used in direct mail sales letters, but it could be used with equal effectiveness on web pages, postcards, and full-page display ads, among others. Here's an example from Steve Manning:

```
┌─────────────────────────────────────────┐
│                                           │
│     Your Next Ad or Marketing Piece       │
│                                           │
│     Isn't Going To Cost You A Dime!       │
│                                           │
│     Because I'm Going to Write It For You │
│                                           │
│          ABSOLUTELY FREE!                 │
│                                           │
└─────────────────────────────────────────┘
```

Frames can come in any number of designs. The lines could be thin or thick. Backgrounds can be shadowed or white and the frame doesn't necessarily need 4 sides. A line on the top and bottom can serve a similar purpose. The traditional *Johnson Box* was actually created long before computers became the standard word processing tool. Back in the days of typewriters, writers didn't have such a luxury. Instead, their frames were created using the asterisk, or another standard symbol on the keyboard.

Setting a frame off to the side can help draw the eye as it appears out of the ordinary. I've created sales letters for clients where only the offer was highlighted within the frame itself. The rest of the headline remained outside the box, but as the largest section of type. The strong offer fit it well and deserved attention all by itself.

Another simple, but proven technique is to place your headline between quotation marks. Testing has indicated that a headline that appears as a direct quotation out-pulls an identical headline that's employed without the quotation marks. But if other people in your market are already doing it, any effect loses its impact. It would seem that many folks place greater credence in words that appear to be from someone else, rather than the marketers and therein lies the power of this simple device.

In the case of marketing headlines, the implication is that those words have come from a satisfied customer. It's certainly worth a test to determine if this simple idea improves your results. Try it. You may be pleasantly surprised, although this technique isn't as effective as it used to be, due to wider use.

Key Points and Simple Design Concepts That Can Dramatically Improve The Impact and Results Of Your Headlines

Design a headline that visually leaps off the page. Make your headline big and bold so it's obvious to everyone. Create a jarring contrast. Present your headline as a few dominant words that are optically interruptive -- like a visual speed-bump that's impossible to miss.

Enhance headlines with photographs or cartoons that add visual spice while complimenting and supporting the text. Combine your headline with a dramatic visual to make your declaration of a benefit easier for prospects to visualize and understand in an instant.

Review every headline from a designer's perspective. Even the strongest-worded headline may be overlooked if it isn't inviting to the eye.

Make your headline the most visually dominating text component. The look or design of a headline can often be its most arresting element. Think of your headline as a big, bold introduction that clearly and succinctly delivers an interesting and inviting statement.

Utilize your allotted space effectively. For small space ads, devote a large percentage to creating a dominant headline. Make your attention-getting headline a large part of your display ad or marketing document. You want to make it obvious and impossible to disregard.

Place your headline inside a call-out, caption, or balloon attached to a graphic. It's a visual stopper that naturally draws the eye and has a good chance of attracting plenty of interest. This technique gives any headline a fighting chance.

Look for additional opportunities to use headlines. On visual pieces such as display ads and brochures, there's often additional space available for secondary headlines. Captions and call-outs naturally attract attention and therefore, are ideal places to insert headline copy. Additional headlines and sub-headings can also be used to provide visual relief by breaking up longer sections of copy. Material that appears easy to read, gets read much more.

Place your headline where your prospect cannot miss it. The best place for any headline is the very first area your prospect's eyes land when turning a page or opening the mail. Keep your headline at *eye level*. You greatly improve your chances of getting noticed.

Position your headline apart from others visually. Your message and the image it projects, should be completely different from all your direct and indirect competitors. View what others are doing and then create an original concept and presentation. This is vitally important whenever your headline is competing with others in the same venue, such as the Yellow Pages. Sometimes an uncultivated, unpolished look may be favorable. This may be your best option when your competitors have taken a slick, professional approach.

Avoid fancy typefaces that make reading difficult. The best typefaces or fonts are very clear and easy to read. Some typefaces only draws attention to themselves and away from your message. Select one that fits the style and substance of your communication -- just make sure it's clearly readable. When printing, choose only light-colored, or white paper stock, with black or another dark ink.

Use enough white space to effectively "frame" your headline so it stands out among the various elements on the page and subtly conveys its' importance. Consider using other framing devices like quotation marks and text boxes that suggest a certain significance to the key words contained within. But most importantly, allow plenty of surrounding space so your headline isn't crammed in.

Employ graphic enhancements such as underlining, bold text, and uppercase lettering, wherever it's appropriate. Dramatizing specific words and phrases causes readers to give these words special attention and importance. An option like reverse type (white text on a solid black background) used in conjunction with a large, bold typeface can make your headline stand out. The key is to use these tools with restraint. A little emphasis goes a long way.

Mix upper and lowercase type. A combination of the two, usually works best for headlines. Avoid using all uppercase type -- it's too difficult to read. Never vary the size of type within the main headline itself.

Chapter 11

How To Write Powerful Headlines
For The Web

"People go through life with their minds only half turned on, except when they're promised an adequate reward for their full attention. Ordinarily their attitude toward nearly everything they see, read and experience is -- so what?"

Maxwell Sackheim

Your main headline is the first thing visitor's see when they arrive at your sales page – at least that's the way it should be. But unfortunately for many web marketers and their respective audiences, that's not the case. Too many web pages are cluttered with over-sized headers and video screens, regulating the headline to a secondary position.

But we've already determined that your headline is number one in your marketing arsenal. So your best headline should take center stage. It's your first and perhaps only opportunity to pull true prospects into your sales copy -- where they can get the full story.

Headlines can and should be used on every individual page of your site. It doesn't matter what the page is about, or whether you're selling or simply providing content. You want visitors to stick around because that's the only way to optimize the traffic you attract.

For the purposes of our discussion here, we'll stick primarily to headlines for online sales letters.

Headlines reveal what you have to offer. They represent the culmination of the finest, most attention-getting, interest-arousing arguments you can muster. It's your best attempt to capture the visitor's brief attention and fuel it into an intense interest. You want them to continue reading as they subconsciously build the desire within to own whatever product or service you're offering.

You've got to get them involved in absorbing your message.

If your headline fails to magnetize prospects, the rest of your sales effort is completely irrelevant because they won't stay long. It really doesn't matter how stellar or persuasive your copy is. If the headline fails to draw an audience, all other efforts to influence, persuade and win the sale are in vain. Without an interested and attentive audience you won't get the opportunity to deliver your pitch and without a convincing pitch you won't make many sales.

With such a significant role assigned to the headline, it stands to reason that headline creation demands a significant investment in time and effort. The trick is to create more riveting headlines than you can ever use on one web page.

The key is to start with a bang. Launch your sales effort with all you've got. Hold nothing back.

You need to give it your absolute best shot in order to grab the attention of your target prospect and have them spend what precious few moments they have with you. There's no room for anything but your best, most magnetic appeal and this is what you need to communicate in the headline.

Since your headline is crucial to your success, it only stands to reason that the headline deserves visual prominence. It should be the first thought your visitor processes upon arrival. You want your headline to jump out instantly – just as quickly as the page loads on the screen of their computers.

Think of your headline as a marquee at the theatre… or a billboard along a busy country road. Place your headline in lights where it's sure to be seen by interested prospects as they speed down the highway of life.

Your HEADLINE is all you've got.

Command interest and you've got a shot at making a sale down the road. Fail to momentarily interrupt the mental trance they're in and visitors will pass your site the same way they pass the coffee shop that has no obvious signage and can't be seen from the roadway.

The Purpose of Web Headlines

Capturing attention, flagging targeted prospects and luring them deep inside your sales copy or content pages are the main functions of web headlines.

To accomplish these tasks, your headline should target your best prospects... be benefit-oriented... make complete sense immediately... and hint at special something that soon follows. Headlines need to be both interesting and promising to the visitor. You've got to give people what they want or they'll be gone as quick as a click.

Grabbing attention is step number one. You need to stop the swift-moving prospect in his tracks and get him to raise an eyebrow or drop a jaw. In other words, you need to penetrate the mental filters with something that immediately hits the sweet spot.

Your web headline has to stop prospects from scanning... grab their attention... trigger an emotional reaction and led them deep into your content. And it has to do it all instantly.

But the major challenge online is to thwart your prospect's temptation to click away. Surfers know that the instant they tire, grow bored of a site, or their interest fades ever so slightly -- all they have to do is click a button to resume their search for feelings of instant gratification elsewhere. When this happens -- as it often does in the click-happy online world -- you lose.

Stopping prospects cold is important. But simply drawing attention from anyone won't be of any real benefit to you.

You want to capture the attention of interested, qualified, and preferably ready-to-buy prospects. Not everyone is a prospect for your offer, despite what you might have been told at one of those internet marketing pitch-fests or multi-level marketing rallies. That's why it's so important to target your message. You want to identify early on, the specific kind of audience your words are best meant to reach. You've got to convince them to stay on your page.

Capturing the attention of non-prospects is of no direct cash value – now or in the future. If the interest simply isn't there, they won't stay long enough to purchase. Focus your marketing efforts on those people who are an ideal match for your offer. Market your solution to those with the specific problem your product can resolve. This is your optimum target and it's what you want to point your site towards.

Flag target prospects in your headline and they'll perk up and listen to what you have to say. Why? They'll listen because you're speaking their language. It's as though you're broadcasting and they're tuned in to your signal. Your message is in resonance with their mindset.

Identify the specific market you've decided to address. Often a single word added to your headline does the job. Your market might be internet marketers, writers, teachers, quilters, California resort owners, seniors, or single mom entrepreneurs – any one of a million different possibilities. Add the label that fits -- the one that whispers in their ear -- and it acts like an unstoppable magnet that pulls in anyone associated with the group.

You might think that you don't need to flag your prospect. After all, your lead-generating marketing is only addressed towards prospective customers. But online, people will find you through various means as your site traffic log will prove. Your offer is geared towards a definable group and those people are the only ones who will buy anyway. So why not communicate with precision and speak only to those you can effectively serve?

Search engines play a large role and the more you actively promote your site and your business, the more accessible your message becomes to the many millions online -- around the world. It makes good sense to let people know who you can help the most. To think that everyone is a potential candidate is simply ludicrous. Narrow your market and your message stands a far greater chance of getting noticed by that specific group. Successful online marketing is targeted marketing.

Here are some examples of headlines that flag specific targets or niches:

"Investors! Make More Money In The Next 45 Days With This New, Fast & Easy System For Organizing, Planning & Tracking All Your Investments In Just 27 Minutes A Day!"

***

Dog Lovers! Show Your Love and Admiration For The "Special Friend" Who Shares Your World... With A Magnificent, Heirloom-Quality Oil Painting... Capture Your Happiest Memories Forever -- With A Hand-Painted, 100% Original Portrait Of Your Precious Pet!

***

"Attention entrepreneurs, small business owners and anyone who has ever dreamed of running their own successful business... New Sure-fire Business Success Library Reveals Breakthrough Tips, Techniques And Secrets For Boosting Sales... Cash Flow... And Profits... Starting Today! Satisfaction Guaranteed 100% -- Or Your Money Back!"

***

If you like good food and discovering new dishes and cuisines, but you're not exactly 'chef material' yourself – here's...

How To Enjoy A Variety Of Fresh, Delicious and Exotic Restaurant-Quality Gourmet Foods – Without Ever Leaving Home!

Introducing... Heavenly Spices -The Lightening-Fast Way To Turn Everyday Foods Into Sizzling Taste Sensations and Delicious Gourmet Meals! It's Fun, Easy, Healthy, and Surprisingly Inexpensive With My Freshly Packed, Hand-Roasted Blends Of 11 Different Herbs And Spices

It's really not that difficult. You simply set out to command attention, identify your audience and woo these people inside. Temporarily stop them in their tracks as they navigate the web at a rapid speed and compel true prospects to stay on your site because you've got something of vital importance – *just for them.*

It's not enough to get the attention of the general public. Your headline only delivers when it pulls qualified prospects deep inside your sales copy. That's the thing. Your headline works if they read on with *interest* and *enthusiasm*. Then the task is to keep adding fuel to the fire until they take the action you want them to take.

What makes online prospects read beyond the headline? It's the promise of a payoff... something of specific interest and importance to your reader. It's a solution, a new or better way to accomplish a task, fulfill a dream, or to solve a worrisome problem. In short, it's about specific benefits being offered to a precisely identified target.

Why Headlines On Web Pages Are So Important

In the online world of endless choice and opportunity, headlines are like signs. They're indicators of what a site or page contains. And in that short message -- often interpreted subconsciously in a split second – lies the ability to pull potential buyers in *now...* or to push them away *forever.*

Headlines are perfect tools to capture the eyes of skimming readers. That's how most people get their information online these days; they click, arrive at a site, and then quickly scan the page looking for items of specific interest and relevance. When they don't find what they're looking for, they click again and again, traveling through cyberspace as fast as they can.

You have one shot at attracting prospects, so the headlines you use to get traffic and to monetize that traffic are critical to your results.

For the online consumer or surfer, headlines are a terrific tool. They reveal (or should reveal) what a site or page is all about.

Picture a web page without a headline or title of any kind. How do you know what's there? You don't. At least, not without reading some of the body copy. But not many people are willing to take the time to do this. After all, why bother? In this day and age where free time seems increasingly difficult to come by and something almost everyone would like more of, any page or site without a compelling "label" is going to be quickly deserted.

Time is precious. Consumer choices are multiplying exponentially. There are multiple demands on everyone's time. For many, it's a never ending merry-go-round. It seems like there's so much to do… and precious little time to do it.

Yet everyone is looking for something to make their life a little better... a little easier... a little less problematic. What is your prospect thinking about? ***This is the ongoing conversation you want to tap into*** *with your headline.*

Placing a targeted headline at the top of your page serves busy people. It catches eyeballs and reveals key information to those who are skimming the surface, hoping to find waters worth swimming in.

This principle can apply to any page on any site. With a strong, descriptive headline front and center, you provide a service that helps visitors and saves them time. The headline tips them off. It immediately reveals the subject matter and relative importance, so the individual can make a snap decision whether the page is worth their time, or at least justifies further investigation.

In the online world, people travel at record speed. Your headline serves the speeding prospect by revealing at a glance what you have to offer and why they should stick around. But with unlimited options only a click away, you need to lay it all on the line – right up front.

The Role Benefits and Breakthroughs Play In Headlines

Benefits are essentially meaningful advantages buyers get as a result of using your product. Benefits are what give a product value and meaning. Since benefits are sought after, they tend to penetrate the filtering devices programmed to deflect the 'noise' of endless messages competing for space in the minds and hearts of the market.

Today, virtually everyone is subjected to a non-stop barrage of commercial messages, distractions, and other demands clamouring for attention on any given day. Most of it is ignored as a mechanism of efficiency and survival.

It's chatter we all know exists and it's something most of us try to avoid. It's like thousands of different radio stations communicating simultaneously. Yet each person can only tune into one station at a time. That single station is represented by the current thought residing in the consciousness of the prospect.

Just imagine what life would be like if you could stop and listen to it all. The huge majority of messages would be of no particular interest and there would be little time for anything else. That's where the filtering process comes into play. It allows the individual to shut out 99.9% of the incoming messages and do so automatically, without any conscious effort. So most people (your prospects included) are buzzing about completely oblivious and uninterested in the noise all around.

But there are those messages that each group pays attention to.

The problem is -- you need to be seen in order to be heard. That's why flagging your prospect is such a powerful tool to command the right kind of attention. When combined with something your visitor really wants, you perpetuate a desire to learn more about your offer because of the feeling it instils.

Headlines act as informative titles, helping prospects make the decision to stay or go.

As the dominant, initial focus, the headline is a sign that advertises what is to come. It enables the prospect to make an instant, gut-level decision as to what to do next almost as soon as they arrive at your site. The only messages that get through are those that hit a nerve... and the surest way to do that is with a benefit that solves a specific problem troubling to your prospect.

Benefits address the thought that is foremost on every prospects mind: *"What's In It For Me?"*

If the promised benefit isn't in alignment with your site visitor's interests or thoughts, it makes no impact and is simply relegated to the 'noise' category. But benefits that hit a nerve are right on target, and offer a timely answer -- *cut through the clutter and receive a welcome reception.*

Specific benefits are meaningful to the right targets. Hence, they are given priority because helpful advantages and benefits are what prospects are looking for. No one buys products -- they buy what the product does for them and *what is does* and *how it helps* are BENEFITS.

Give It A New Twist

But if the benefits you present don't appear to be a new breakthrough, your benefit-laden headline might not be enough. What's new about what you have to share?

Inject something new into your benefit headlines. "New" is a breakthrough that hasn't been seen before.

Give them something that was previously unknown, unavailable, or under wraps and hidden to the public. Rock your prospect's world. Today's consumers of information are on the lookout for new products, recent developments, upgrades, and "new and improved" ways of doing just about anything. Adding a degree of newness distinguishes your online offering from all the others.

Test words and terms that convey the concept of a new solution. Some examples include: *revolutionary, now, at last, just arrived, introducing, announcing, suddenly, unleashed, important development, breakthrough, improvement,* and *shocking.*

Get attention with the promise of a strong benefit that's fresh and new. Emphasize your unique angle and what makes it new to distinguish your message from all others.

If it's the same old story, nobody will read on. But add a new spin to it and you raise eyebrows. Arouse curiosity in your web headline and you'll dramatically increase the number of those who read beyond it and spend more time on your site.

A curiosity-inducing headline is difficult to resist because it's like an unanswered question that demands an answer... an itch that simply must be scratched. We are curious by nature and need to find out the rest of the story for ourselves.

How To Get Started Writing Great Headlines For The Web

Begin with research. Research gives you knowledge about your market – something that's a tremendous advantage. The time spent in research gives you everything you need to create a compelling, intriguing headline from scratch -- one that's sure to interest more genuine prospects than a headline created any other way.

The secret is to understand your market. Knowing you audience clues you in to their specific desires and aspirations… as well as their problems, frustrations, and anxieties. These are the things that your prospect is thinking about on a regular basis. These are hot buttons. It's these issues that occupy their minds. Therefore, it's no surprise that when you hit on these in your headline and you offer a specific and much-wanted benefit, you quickly capture an eager and attentive audience.

Delivering a key benefit-oriented headline also means understanding the capabilities of you product and the unique advantages it gives others.

Why would anyone be willing to listen to you if you don't have anything to say that's worth their time and attention? Online prospects won't wait. If you don't provide a key benefit right up front – something that piques their interest and gets the blood rushing a little, you won't stand a chance. It's too easy to avoid the unexciting and unimportant.

Presenting a unique benefit means you're also intimately aware of what others are offering. Take the time to review your competitors. Know what they're doing and what sales tactics they've tried before. If you know your competitor's products thoroughly, you'll understand their strengths and weaknesses. This makes it easier to develop a strategy that positions you in the most favourable light. As the web continues to evolve, new competitors will likely appear on your turf, so it's something you'll want to monitor consistently.

The Most Effective Headline Formats To Use Online

Headlines with sub-headings, multiple benefit, and combination packages work well. Longer, strongly-worded headlines tend to pack more of a punch. Fit your combination headline into the first frame of your sales letter – that's how you maximize the use of your most valuable online real estate. It needs to be "above the fold" so your message is seen without scrolling and delivered in one powerful punch.

The danger in using this kind of headline lies in overdoing it. Avoid excessively long headlines that try to do too much. Your intention is to give them a delicious taste and invite them inside where the buffet awaits. Headlines that work are headlines that keep the prospect interested and involved.

One great advantage of web site marketing is the dirt-cheap price of space. With virtually every other form of advertising, you have a finite amount of real estate and a set fee for the use of this space. Exceed it and it costs you more money. Cost overruns could be the undoing of a marginally profitable campaign.

But in the online world, these limitations don't exist.

You can, in effect, use as much space as you want. Obviously, your message must remain focused and interesting to the reader. But having usable space and making it captivating and alluring are different matters altogether. The low cost of space is inviting… but the challenge is that online – human attention spans appear to be at an all-time low.

Space ads are costly. So too are sizable direct mail campaigns. That's why you need to maximize the value of every square inch of space and every element required in a mailing. Regardless of the size of your ad, the available space allotted the headline is somewhat limited.

In direct mail, you have weight considerations to deal with too. What this usually boils down to is a specific number of pages in which to get your message across. Make your headline any longer and suddenly your eight-page letter turns into a nine-pager. The added cost at the post office could be self-defeating to your advertising campaign.

In cyberspace, these restrictions are effectively lifted -- giving you much more freedom to use a longer headline and pack more punch into your prime property. Your most valuable space is the first "frame" or screen visible to your visitor.

Here are some examples of online sales letter headlines:

If you ever wanted a fully-functional, professionally-designed business (or personal) website of your own, but didn't want to spend hundreds —or thousands— in design fees… than this is for you…

"They Laughed When I Set Out To Build A Professional Quality Website… But Their Laughter Soon Turned To Stunned Silence When I Did It Myself In Just 1 Day – With No HTML, No Special Technical Skills, and No Previous Design Experience Whatsoever"

…NOW it's easier than EVER for anyone – anywhere… to create an exciting, high-value web site and gain an Internet presence virtually overnight… for mere "chump change"

***

Introducing… The All-Natural Bodybuilding System For Gaining Massive Size, Incredible Strength And Awesome Power...

I'll Show You 67 Specific Insider Secrets For Transforming Your Body Into A Finely Sculpted Mass Of Huge, Rock-Solid Muscle --The 100% Safe And Natural Way

***

Fed up with all the deceptive "how-to make money online" garbage out there? Wish you could find just one REAL LEGITIMATE WAY to make REAL MONEY right from your kitchen table – starting today? Well… listen up -- in the next 4 minutes I'll show you...

How To Easily Get Full Cases Of Top Quality, Name-Brand Products At Half The Wholesale Price… And How To Quickly Sell Every Piece At A Huge Profit On EBAY - Hassle-Free And In Less Time Than You Think! My "Amazing" New Book Reveals The Simple Secrets Of How I Average $11,212.00 A Month -- 100% Online!

Finally! Here's Your Direct Roadmap To The Exact Same Highly Profitable -- Yet Exceptionally Easy -- Money Making Techniques I Use Every Day To Make Big Money While At Home With My Kids! I've Never Shared This Information With Anyone – Until Now! Read On And You'll See How My Story Could Just As Easily Be Your Story…

***

Ready for your financial freedom? Here are the exact same methods experts use to create true wealth...

Discover How To Triple Your Investment Success, Eliminate Costly Commissions and Take Total Control Of Your Financial Destiny – Starting Today

Revealed: 37 closely-guarded investment secrets to creating your own personal fortune. Make more money and build lifelong wealth, with greater ease and more confidence than you ever thought possible!

If you like to call your own shots... If you want to build your own personal fortune quietly... methodically... systematically... if you want to take advantage of the incredible technology that's right at your fingertips, now... then, you must read this letter very carefully...

***

How To Create a Powerful Web Headline In Minutes

Keywords that cut to the heart of your prospect's pleasure or pain zone are certain to capture the attention and interest of that specific group. High-value benefits... extra advantages... and unique solutions all naturally draw attention and interest.

To the prospect suffering from a seemingly incurable case of hay fever, a headline such as *"How To Stop Acid Reflux In 33 Seconds With This Secret Ingredient Found In Almost Every Refrigerator!"* is virtually guaranteed to interrupt his online travels and the dozen or so thoughts swirling around in his mind to draw him straight towards your message.

The obvious keyword here is "Acid Reflux" -- this is what the prospect's radar is set to detect. More specifically, it's the cure, or the alleviation of pain and discomfort that the prospect seeks. But it's the use of the keyword itself that identified the message as having importance -- *triggering the reaction and immediate shift in focus.*

Prospects are constantly on the lookout for 'new' ideas, solutions, and upgrades -- hence the common practice among marketers to unveil 'new and improved' versions of older products. 'New' implies an improvement over the old, established way. It hints at the promise of a greater benefit.

But many people turn to the web first for information. It's a handy research tool that puts the world at their fingertips. They're not necessarily "shopping" but your targeted headline can be a powerful lure that pulls them in on your line.

Promise a unique advantage and you increase your chances of drawing an interested audience. As humans, we're wired to spot new ways to get more living out of life. We want more… and we want it faster, easier and at a lower cost. Headlines that scream such advantages generally reap the reward of higher readership. But each and every market niche has its own nuances, so the more you know your market, the more likely you are to connect and make a substantial impact.

Another strategy for creating powerful online headlines is to employ proven, attention-getting words and phrases. Used sparingly, these words work well. Refer to the list provided elsewhere in this book and add to it as you discover other words. Obviously, you'll want to customize your headline to suit the application, but stringing together a few words from this list can get you off to a good start. These words work in direct mail and they work online too in many markets. It's worth testing any "power words" that fit your content.

How To Take a Good Headline and Make It Even Stronger

Guarantees, added incentives and definite deadlines give an added sense of urgency and importance to your headline. A guarantee offers immediate backup for any claim stated previously. You still need to prove your point. But the fact that the promise is *guaranteed* adds power and significance to the message of the headline.

Imagine prospects as they arrive at your site. The first thing they see is your headline.

In your headline, you offer benefit one, benefit two, and benefit three. Benefit #1 seemed impressive... Benefit #2 astonishing. But Benefit #3 has never been offered before by anyone, as far as the prospect is concerned. It seems too good to be true... almost unbelievable. But then you follow up your triple benefit headline with a simple statement like *"Guaranteed 100% Or It Doesn't Cost You A Dime!"*

The guarantee by itself adds credibility and security. Each of the benefits is attractive in its own right. But when combined, you've packaged a loaded statement that's difficult to ignore.

Perception is everything and more often than not, the prospect's perception is that since it's fully guaranteed – your BENEFITS must be true. Now, I'm not suggesting that you misrepresent ANYTHING. Not by a long shot. In fact, I implore you to tell the truth, the whole truth and nothing but the truth. But at the same time… it's your duty to make your offering as interesting and desirable as humanly possible. A guarantee helps you accomplish this by making your statement less of a stretch in the prospect's mind. The prospect reasons -- *"If this was far-fetched, why would you bother to risk such a guarantee and be inundated with returns?"*

Added incentives compel readers because of the value they offer.

When you can pack an appealing "extra" into your headline, you often attract more eyeballs. Free offers of specific importance or added benefits tend to pull larger numbers of targeted prospects. The more lop-sided the value (in favour of the prospect) -- the more appealing your headline and offer becomes. Stack 3 compelling benefits into your headline and you can increase your headline's effectiveness exponentially.

Clearly-stated deadlines add a sense of urgency. It's a hot potato in your prospect's hands -- something he realizes he must deal with now instead of later. Adding a specific expiry date in your headline and combining it with a strong offer gets people interested and activated. They know the material is time-sensitive, so they're forced to check it out right away.

How To Write An Emotional Headline

Touch on the key issues in your prospect's life. Connect with the inner conversation already taking place. Use picture words that trigger strong mental images, while feeding existing desires. Inject emotion into your headline messages and provide your audience the precise solution to alleviating a frustrating and ongoing problem.

There is nothing more seductive, more intriguing, or more appealing to your prospects than a handful of power words that hit them where they live by instantly creating positive and pleasurable feelings.

Desire is a powerful force that can work in your favour. But it first needs to be unleashed. It is therefore, both a challenge and opportunity to awaken this sleeping giant by hitting the right button and presenting a scenario of promise and possibility. If your prospect can relate to the promise and see it as attainable, a strong feeling of confidence washes over, placing the ideal outcome within reach. And it all starts by painting a promising picture that offers hope and inspiration.

What are your prospect's *hot buttons*? What does he really desire? How does that make him feel? How can you ignite these happy feelings in your headline?

Cast a provocative and appealing picture. Offer the kind of result that changes lives. Express your strongest benefits in vivid color. Telegraph an attainable outcome clearly and concisely. Allow your prospect to experience temporary ownership of the actual benefits in his mind's eye. Doing this allows your prospect to instantly make the dramatic transition from his current conditions -- to the ideal result he ultimately seeks.

Here's an example of a standard web headline:

"Create Great Looking Documents With Ease"

Here's a modified version of the same concept – but this one has been brought to life with an infusion of emotion:

> *"Here's Your One and Only Chance To Snag This 7-Time Winner of "Best In Class" Award By PC Software Magazine at 57% Off... and Turn Your Simple Pages Into Beautiful Eye-Catching Messages That Are Simply Impossible To Ignore!"*

You've got it. Now let others in on whatever it is you've got.

The best way to write powerful, emotionally-charged headlines is to get motivated. Prepare yourself mentally. Get fired up first. Know that you have something to offer that can truly change your buyer's life. Get clear in your mind about the benefits, advantages and uniqueness that can be theirs. Then get passionate about your offer.

Inject a new level of enthusiasm and drama into the words you enter on the page. Write as though you have the ultimate answer to your prospect's plight. Do whatever it takes to get your prospect closer to the magical results he yearns for. If what you've got is what is wanted and you communicate it with impact, precision, power and speed – you will pull in the right kind of people in droves.

What Kind of Things Do Successful Web Headlines Offer?

Effective web headlines offer the promise of an advantage or benefit. But not just any advantage will do. For best results, serve up a relevant advantage of utmost importance. Promise something BIG (obviously, something you can deliver on) and something that's sure to please the target market you intend to reach.

Compelling advantages/benefits are the heart and soul of headlines and all sales messages. But that's not the only place to deliver benefits. Even content pages can benefit from a massive increase in readership with the addition of a headline that delivers a much-desired benefit.

Differentiate your offer from all others. Anytime you can offer a strongly desired benefit that's *new,* something that *requires little effort,* yet is *guaranteed* to produce satisfaction -- you've got even more to offer.

Benefits need to offer unique solutions or unexploited angles. What is it that sets your offer apart from someone else selling the same kind of thing? If your product is truly unique, by all means promote this distinction and claim it as your own. Stand tall and use what separates your offer from all others to your advantage.

But if you happen to be in a market that's filled with competing products making similar claims, all is not lost. Simply find a unique, underused advantage and use this single aspect as the foundation upon which you can build a strong, attention-grabbing headline. This strategy gives you an authentic and original position in the minds of your consumers. It's about taking an overlooked, but often common advantage and giving it special attention, thereby creating the appearance of exclusivity.

Simplify life for your audience by offering a solution that's both quick and easy to apply.

In today's society, time is our most precious resource. So whenever you can offer a time-saving bonus and feature it in your headline -- you should. Your prospects and customers work long and hard. They're pulled this way and that way. By the end of the day, they're exhausted – physically and mentally. It's only after they do what they have to do that they even have time to venture out online.

Now imagine your prospect searching the web for information.

Various details and apparent answers are available, but most require an investment of time, energy and focus. But it's the end of another long day, so those personal resources of time, energy and focus are in short supply. Suddenly, your prospect arrives at your site where your headline leaps off the screen. It offers a quick-fix for whatever ails them. Not only that -- it's virtually effort-free.

Deliver this kind of a punch and your headline is simply too irresistible to pass up. Your prospect is captivated from the start… giving you a much better chance of eventually making the sale.

Now if you can guarantee a particular result, that's even better. But if you're going to mention your guarantee in the headline, it should be a powerful, 'no holds barred' type of guarantee -- a guarantee with teeth. *(Please note: You need to add the appropriate disclaimers to meet FTC regulations and any other that may or may not apply.)*

Pack a punch. The single most important thing your online headline can deliver is a relevant benefit. Ideally, your BIG benefit is one that no one else can match. If it fits, you can also add the promises of fast action, convenience and the assurance of a 100% guarantee.

Here it is in one simple formula:

Big NEW Benefit + Quick & Easy Solution + Guaranteed Satisfactory Results = Powerful Web Headline

Here are some examples of multiple-promise headlines:

"RETAILERS: Sell More Suits At Full Price TODAY Than You've Ever Sold In A Single Day Before. Remarkable New ABC Technique Fills Your Store With Customers Eager To Buy More Suits, Shirts, Dress Pants, and Ties Than Ever… And At Full Price – Satisfaction Guaranteed!"

***

Ontario Man Forced At "Wife-Point" To Clean Up The Clutter and Unload Massive Collection of Advertising Gems – OR ELSE -- means you get to legally "steal" from the best...

Here's Your Rare Chance To Own An Enormous, 15+ Pound Swipe File Featuring Brilliant Ads, Sales Letters, Direct Mail Pieces, and More From Marketing Geniuses and Copywriting Wizards like Jay Abraham, Dan Kennedy, Gary Halbert, Bob Bly... at a Near Give-Away Price. I Guarantee You Won't Find This Powerful Package Anywhere Else.

***

"How To Create Your Own Hot, Best-Selling Information Product On Your Favourite Subject In Less Than 3 Hours – Guaranteed 100%!"

***

"Want To Write Copy That Can Make You Rich? Here's My GUARANTEED, Market-Tested, A-Z Formula For Writing Words That SELL -- Plus $979 Worth Of FREE BONUSES -- If You're One Of The First 47 People To Respond To This One-Time-Only Offer!"

Where Else Do These Headline Ideas Apply?

Headlines are the single most important component of any type of marketing - period. Headline opportunities abound in the online world. You can apply many of these ideas to any of your promotional activities including forum and discussion board postings and identification, web page title tags that are viewed by search engines, directory listings, article titles, content pages, squeeze pages, and ezine ads, and more.

Whenever you get the opportunity to attract the interest and attention of your target audience, it behooves you to employ what is unquestionably your single most effective tool. The headline is the key to getting your message noticed by the right people in virtually any arena.

Key Points To Keep In Mind When Creating Online Sales Letter Headlines

Target your ideal prospect with a compelling and concise statement designed to arrest attention and fuel interest. That's what headlines are all about. It's your first and only chance to woo prospects in -- and getting them beyond that first step is crucial to your success.

Use your most alluring appeal to capture the attention and interest of your niche audience. Don't hold back. Avoid saving the best for last and instead jump out of the gate with your biggest guns firing.

If you don't use your most powerful advantage upfront -- as the first thing prospects see -- they'll never take the time to read beyond your headline.

Online prospects are busy people. Much of the time they're on a mission to find specific information pertinent to their needs and wants at the time. Never forget that. They won't give you a second chance in their search for desired details and resources that will move them closer to their goals.

To grab attention and get people out of the trance they're in, you've got to be different. Using the same words and making the same claims as everyone else probably won't be of much help to you. You prospective customer sees such an approach as simply more of the same.

You need something unique… something with a fresh spin… something that sets you apart in a big way from the other guys.

You need a headline that's riveting… one that demonstrates a clear understanding of your market and the unmet want it's had to endure – until now. You need a headline that captures minds and hearts so they continue to read with an increased level of emotional involvement.

Employ your strongest advantage. If your offer can't be beat – say so. If your benefits are unmatched through traditional means – by all means, vault that message to the top of your page. Present your strongest appeal and you'll maximize readership, subscriptions, positive feedback and of course – sales.

It's the job of the headline to capture the eyeballs of your target audience and deliver enough enticement to lure them into your copy. Ultimately, you want to gently, comfortably and naturally lead your target customers to the order form and encourage them to buy.

Make it captivating, compelling, and as concise as you can. But don't make your web headlines short for the sake of saving space. You've got plenty of space within that first screen of your site. Make it count by getting visitors to stay and spend more time with you.

Be different. Do the unexpected. Refine your biggest bang down to a handful of words that are sure to arrest attention, arouse curiosity and ignite desire.

Compose your best headline and put it out there.

Be sure to measure your response with each exposure. Test a different version and see how it stacks up to the original. It's likely that some results will be expected, while others will completely floor you. The only way to know for sure is to test.

Simple Enhancements To Make Your Web Site Headline Impossible To Miss

Drawing the prospect's attention to your headline is job one. To accomplish this task, place your headline where people expect to find it – right at the top of your page. Sounds obvious. But this simple point is often ignored in favour of large graphics, videos and page headers. There may be a place for these elements on your web site. But why compromise the effect of your strongest, most-compelling message and risk losing out altogether?

Here's something else you'll want to do: create an obvious visual contrast between your headline and body copy.

Make your web headline big and bold. If your body copy is set in 12-point type, place your headline in 18-point or 20-point type. Make the difference noticeable. Avoid using a look that's virtually the same -- such as 11-point body copy with a 12-point headline. It's a minor difference that's barely distinguishable. Large headlines in bold type communicate significance, so eyes are naturally drawn towards them.

Experiment with the type size and style of your headline. A key point to remember is to get your main headline to appear in its entirety -- within the opening frame. By doing so, you direct your visitor's focus towards the juiciest carrot you can offer. Make your headline fit and make it clearly legible so visitors can easily read, understand and be completely consumed by your message -- so they don't leave. Your headline is the key to the next action they take.

Try setting your headline in bold type. Does it still fit the frame? Is it clear and easy to read? If so, use it. Bold text establishes a position of prominence and importance. It signals to the reader that this particular segment is something of significance -- something that must be seen.

Create a headline that calls out to your niche audience in a way that must be noticed. Be sure that it's clear, easy to read, and centered on the page with adequate balance.

Headlines set in big, bold type attract attention first, as the eye is naturally drawn towards large, dark objects. Anything that stands out ... anything different from the typical text on a page tends to pull the eye towards it. It's a natural reaction and one that's difficult to avoid even with concentrated effort. Now go out and use this information to your advantage.

How Can You Be Sure Your Web Headline Works Effectively?

The only measure of success in any marketing endeavour is the result produced.

You can have what you think is the best headline, sales letter, presentation, product, price, etc. But it's all academic. You can follow all the guidelines in the world and still come up short. There's no panacea; no one-size-fits-all answer that will ensure your headline's success in the real world – online or offline.

The only way to know for sure is to put it to the test.

Follow these ideas. Apply them. Take action and get your headlines out there in front of the marketplace where response is the only way to measure the actual effectiveness of your efforts.

You've got to be willing to test and test again. That's the only way to accurately determine your most effective headlines. By following these techniques, you'll easily triple your chances of success. But you've still got to let the market decide. Give it your best shot and then get it out there. Test it and tweak it. Then test again.

The best way to create one strong headline is to write several. Begin by jotting down a few headline ideas. You can always add to your list later. If you can write a dozen different headlines, chances are that somewhere within your list of twelve, there lies a gem of a headline waiting to be brought forth and used for maximum impact. At times it works best to combine several elements from different headlines. This is a proven way to make a good headline even better because these revamped versions tend to read smoother than those off-the-cuff suggestions.

Choosing one headline from many can be a challenging task. Best thing to do is to imagine yourself as the prospect for your offer. Step into the role of the individual you're trying to reach. Then examine each headline through your prospect's eyes.

Does it grab you?

What words catch your eye and push your hot buttons?

When writing headlines -- let the ideas flow. Don't set out to craft the perfect headline at once, or you'll only get frustrated. Instead, write down whatever compelling words and phrases come to mind that best describe what you have to offer.

Group some of these words together and shape what you have into a headline. When you've written several, step back and try to single out the strongest 2-3 headline variations from your list. Take the elements that make the most dramatic impact and reshape, repackage, or recast them into a new version – a hybrid headline. That's an important secret to creating a headline with the potential pulling power of a blockbuster.

When you've narrowed it down to a main headline you think will work for your online sales letter, test it in the classifieds. Run your classified ad in the largest daily newspaper you can. In this ad, use nothing more than your strongest, most promising headline and your web site address or URL. If you've got a high-traffic website elsewhere, you can display your new product headline there and measure the number of clicks it gets.

If the headline alone can draw clicks from a tiny classified ad in a print publication, chances are you've got a winner. The reason? You're relying solely on the headline to stimulate enough interest so prospects make a note of your URL and take the time to visit your site. If you patiently wait for the next print edition of your targeted publication to appear – that will likely give you the most relevant and accurate results. But even newspaper classifieds can worthwhile places to test headlines – though I generally don't suggest them as an effective choice when you're marketing to specific niches.

Another way to test headlines is to set up two identical pages with the exact same content, except for the headline. Run two different versions and split test your ads 50/50 so you get virtually the same exposure to each unique URL.

Since traffic will vary, pay particular attention to your conversion rates. Measure the response. You may be surprised by what you discover. Again, the only way to know with absolute certainty is to test your marketing and the first and often most revealing test is the headline variety. Everything is mere theory until it's tested fairly and measurably in the marketplace.

How Long Should Your Web Headline Be?

Make your headline long enough to deliver a compelling message... and short enough to be consumed in one gulp. Limit the length of your headline to something that can be scooped up and understood, without the need to come up for air.

Your headline should deliver a powerful and interest-arousing thought that tempts, teases, and tantalizes enough to win over more of the prospect's time. That's really what it's all about. Pull them in instead of pushing them away. You want to stimulate emotional desire. Get their minds thinking about new promises and possibilities.

Give them a taste of what can be theirs... and leave the door open so they can find out more. Once a seed is planted into a receptive mind, your prospects will find themselves driven to get the whole story. They want answers – essentially a form of closure. Tempt them and you stir up long-forgotten desires. But once activated and agitated, they become determined to get more information to satisfy their curiosity.

Deliver a benefit-laden message and claim the space you require. Don't be afraid to string a few benefits together to create an even stronger effect. Here's an example:

Congratulations... 30 days from now you could have your own thriving Scrapbooking business... you can work your own hours from home... wake when you want... revolve it around family commitments - and take control of your financial destiny once and for all doing something you LOVE! (Brett McFall)

If you attempt to tease prospects with hype, while short-changing them on information in the hope that they'll read on to get the full scoop, it could backfire. Decisions online are made in an instant. Give it your best shot without any delay. But be clear about what it is you're offering. It's the only way to demonstrate a healthy respect for other people's time.

With so many choices available, today's online prospect won't spend extra time trying to figure out if what you're offering is worth his attention. A better strategy is to be explicit in the beginning – starting with your headline.

Blind headlines are a definite no-no. Instead, give readers what they want. Make it worth their time to consume your headline message and rekindle a deep desire. Do that and you increase your chances that they'll stay awhile.

The foundation of a solid online headline can be explained in one sentence: Unleash your ultimate benefit or advantage and make it as interesting, special and appealing as you possibly can.

Your headline's purpose is to get your IDEAL PROSPECT to pay attention and to focus on your sales copy with enthusiasm and interest. Give yourself adequate space to accomplish this goal. If you need more room to fully deliver the ultimate refinement of what you offer, add a sub-head... or use an introductory super-headline to set up your main message. Make it flow together seamlessly and deliver a compelling message true prospects will find impossible to ignore.

Make your headline short enough to be understood at a glance. This allows you to capture the skimming reader and deliver a compelling and magnetic message at the same time.

The Realities of Communicating Online

Most people watch television for entertainment purposes. They read magazines and newspapers to discover news of interest. But they venture out online first and foremost for information. They know *information* can be found on virtually any topic, event, or product. Buying online usually isn't their primary intention – at least not initially. Gathering important details is step one.

As your typical surfer logs on, they do so with a particular subject in mind. It could be anything at all such as a cure for acid reflux, tips on writing a resume, or how to build a backyard deck. Whatever it is that your prospects are thinking about and tuned into – that's exactly what you need to address in your headline.

But they're on the outside looking in. Browsing is easy online and until they decide to check out your page in more detail, they're only window shopping. More often than not, the deciding factor is your headline.

Your web headline needs to reach out and touch those who can benefit from what you have to offer. It needs to make a connection. You don't want to tell the whole story... just enough to get them hooked on spending extra time to get more information.

But the reality is that it's easier to click away than it is to stay.

Clicks are quick and easy and require no mental effort whatsoever. Besides, they've already got their finger on the trigger. That's why you need to deliver a magnetic message on the spot, or miss the chance to deliver your complete sales presentation.

In the unlimited and often anonymous online world, it's easy to mindlessly surf by skimming, scrolling and clicking. It doesn't require much focus or mental energy. And nothing can interrupt the trance except a headline that goes straight to the prospect's brain with a clear and personally-addressed message that screams -- *"This is for me!"*

What stops them cold is the message contained in your well-positioned headline.

In the online word, judgements are made in an instant and rarely, if ever are they reconsidered. People are used to processing the perceived content of web pages quickly and making instantaneous decisions based on the first few words they encounter upon arrival.

Since your headline determines whether visitors stay or click away, it's the headline that needs to take center stage. It's the focal point.

Your headline needs to be obvious when your visitors first come in for a landing. If it's not, your leaving it up to whatever is visible on the page and nothing can communicate with the pulling power of a precision-targeted and hard-hitting headline.

Ultimately, you want visitors to continue reading your copy to the point where they decide to buy. So every sentences needs to at the very least, sustain their current level of interest. That's why it's a good idea to mix up your sales pages with a combination of text boxes, bullet points, short, and one-line paragraphs.

Most importantly, you'll want to sprinkle in a healthy serving of extra headlines throughout your pages. These sub-heads act as powerful, interest-fuelling messages designed to keep prospects actively involved and excited about what's in store for them.

Employ these sub-heads at every opportunity and infuse them with the same kind of appeal you'd pack into any important headline. Begin every text box, callout, sign-up form, testimonial, or table with a headline of its own.

Vivid, descriptions and strong verbs draw prospects inside. When you paint a word picture related to a desired outcome, it creates a pleasurable "aha!" feeling that captures minds and hearts.

Visitors sense right away if your page is holds immense promise, or if they'd be better off seeking those positive emotions elsewhere.

Headlines can be intriguing, inspiring, or controversial. They can make a big, bold claim or promise, arouse curiosity, or deliver important news. However you write them, what really matters is what your visitors do next. If they flee, your headline has failed. But if they remain on your site to get more information, your headline has succeeded.

Chapter 12

Writing Successful Press Release Headlines

"Your headline is everything! Spend more time on your headline than the entire rest of the release. The only job your headline has is to suck the reporter in and force him to keep reading. If the headline doesn't do its job, the rest of your release could be phenomenal, but it won't get read."

Paul Hartunian

When it comes to press releases, headlines play a crucial role -- just as they do in all forms of advertising and marketing communications.

Press release headlines need to:

1. Capture attention...
2. Target a specific audience... and...
3. Trigger a desire in the recipient to read on immediately.

But that's where the similarities to typical headlines end.

If you use a "marketing" headline -- your news release will be instantly trashed. When you think about it, this makes perfect sense. After all, press releases are meant for editors and reporters and these people have a job to do. Their mission is to seek out new interesting stories for their respective audiences. To do this, they rely on a fresh batch of news releases on their fax machines, in their in-boxes, on press release web sites and by mail and courier services too.

Technological advances have spawned the growth of many web-based services. Wire services and publicity sites that host press releases have made it possible for writers and editors to "shop" for relevant news items. They don't have to wait to see what comes in. The can quickly scan new releases as they're posted.

Since many of these sites have thousands of listings, with more releases coming in all the time, they're categorized by title only. This means that virtually every list shows nothing but the HEADLINE.

It's the "label principle" at work here. The label or headline is your only hope to capture the interest and imagination of members of the media. That's why you need to nail it in as few words as possible.

The headline on your release needs to pull like a magnet. You've got to deliver an intriguing story of particular interest -- so they can grasp it in a rapid fly-by. A nearly instantaneous decision is made whether to pursue the story or pass on it.

What's Different About Press Release Headlines?

Editors and veteran reporters know the game. They understand that you're in business and your intentions are to capture some publicity for your business, product, event, or cause. That's perfectly fine. These folks count on receiving heaps of releases, in the hope that the odd gem appears.

But publicity seekers need to understand that editors and journalists aren't in the game to help sell goods or promote any predetermined agenda. Their primary obligation is to please their readers, viewers, or listeners. Since they're on the prowl for new and interesting information, they accept press releases as potential leads for stories. But they object vehemently to blatant marketing that doesn't follow the generally accepted formula they favour and are used to.

However, as long as you play by the rules, you're usually good to go. Free publicity can pay off in spades because *people generally accept what that media says*. It's this perceived endorsement that makes the small effort required well worth it.

Play to win. But understand the challenges involved as you go and the number one challenge is to get a fair reading of your release. All you've got are words on a page, or pixels on a screen and about a second or two to pass the first critical test.

This is where your headline comes in. It has to reach out and grab the reader by the collar and force them to take note of your message. You need a line of text as your headline that's a certain "grabber".

Nothing is more important to the results achieved from your publicity efforts than your press release headline. It reveals important clues about your "story". If your headline message doesn't appeal to the receiving editor/reporter, you're dead in the water.

That's just the way it is.

Picture an editor pouring over today's stack of press releases. Yours is in there somewhere, buried amongst hundreds of others crafted by people with similar intentions.

But there's only so much time in the day to develop a story and sculpt it into useable format. So the first hurdle your release has to pass is the waste basket. Imagine the editor sifting through a stack of releases while standing over the trash. Decisions are made instantly, at first glance. Your *news* has to swiftly command attention, triggering a double-take.

What determines whether your release gets any more than a few seconds of an editor's time? It's the headline, of course.

The One Task of the Headline

Capturing the attention and interest of the target recipient is the principle job of the headline. Your headline needs to get past the gatekeeper... stop editors (and/or staff) in their tracks... and interrupt their thought processes long enough to pass. You want them to keep your release in the "A" pile and away from the trash, where inevitably 99% of all releases are headed.

A strong headline gets you in the game. It opens the door to free publicity that could be worth a fortune to a growing business.

Your on-target headline gives you a fighting chance at media coverage -- whether that takes the form of a feature article, interview, radio exposure, or a published review of your product. The potential benefits of free publicity are enormous and the number one secret to success is to craft an irresistible headline.

Think of the headline at the top of the page as a stoplight. You're captured attention briefly. But whether they advance or turn away depends on the impact of your words.

Busy editors may assign the task of sifting and sorting releases to others, with strict requirements about what they're looking for. They do so because they realize from experience that much of what is submitted simply isn't a good fit for their purposes and they get far more press releases than they could ever use. Since it's a time-consuming process to evaluate submissions regularly, this task is assigned to a subordinate. It's this individual who in essence becomes the gatekeeper, providing an additional filtering mechanism to weed out the unfit or irrelevant, helping minimize the consumption of the organization's over-stretched resources.

Expect to have your press release scrutinized. Since most of what's received isn't exactly what the media outlet wants, your release is immediately suspect. Your message is generally perceived as unfit or unqualified from the outset -- and it's up to you to overcome this bias in the blink of an eye.

This is where your headline comes into play. It's why the headline is the single most important component. In one line you immediately communicate the *relevance, importance* and *newsworthiness* of your message.

What qualifies as "news" or a "newsworthy" item? Anything *new* is news -- as long as it's relevant to the market. News is always action-based and timely. In other words -- it's something of importance to readers, listeners, or viewers right now.

This sense of immediacy conveyed in the headline makes your release a hot potato in the hands of your target recipient. It commands instant attention, draws serious interest and captures the imagination of those you reach. It forces them to keep reading as you make a positive first impression on the minds of these busy editors scurrying about looking for their next story.

Related news that serves their customer base will get noticed -- if you communicate this effectively in your headline.

If your headline fails, anything else you've written won't matter matter one bit. The headline must lead them into reading the full page. If you fail here, they'll never recast your story in their own words and present it to their respective audiences. Generating media interest is a crucial preliminary step. You have to first win them over if you are to succeed in your publicity efforts.

The Foundation of an Effective Press Release

Press releases should be crafted for the editor/reporter's eyes. But they also need to be perfectly suited to the ultimate consumer of that information too. You have to get those in the media to hear you out. That's the first and absolutely necessary step to having your story told to the public. But to achieve this mission, you need to tailor your approach differently.

There are two things that separate successful, publicity-seeking headlines from all others and it's this:

1. *You must convey NEWS or information that is truly NEWSWORTHY.* It should read like a compelling headline at the top of a red-hot story that's fresh.

2. *You need to inject a sense of ACTION.* Using an effective verb brings your headline to life.

Additionally, you need to stimulate their curiosity with something unique. Differentiate yourself. Add an original twist that separates your message from others.

To capture hearts and minds, your story needs to be more interesting, intriguing, or important to the media outlet's consumers than the other 147 releases stacked high on the editor's desk.

You've got to think like a reporter... get inside his head... and push the right buttons. Supply the crucial information he wants -- exactly the way he wants it. And there's no better way to cut to the chase than with a headline that's impossible to ignore.

Media outlets thrive on *news* because that's what consumers hunger for. It's why people listen to talk radio, watch interview-type television, and read newspapers, magazines and trade publications pertinent to their interests and occupations.

Every writer and editor needs a steady supply of fodder, so they pick through a bunch of releases hoping to discover something fresh, hot, exciting and interesting... something they know their audience will eagerly eat up. In competitive markets, every editor wants to be first to get the scoop, or to snag an exclusive story and reveal it to their own customers.

Actions of Significance

So the primary qualification of the press release headline is to communicate news of interest to the target audience. Give them a nugget with story potential -- something that has happened, or is about to. Effective "news" headlines are action-oriented, with a sense of immediacy about them. They get right to the point too. Without a newsworthy angle, your *news release* is meaningless.

It can be as simple as unveiling a new product and what it does for others. Your product is NEWS – what it does for other people represents its meaningful BENEFIT VALUE.

Know what readers, listeners, or viewers LOVE and deliver it with a bang. Offer a solution to a big problem that has yet to be resolved.

It's best to provide just the bait. But you'll have to do so in the most interesting way possible. Don't tell the full story. Get the media interested or curious enough to investigate the possibility of doing a full story based on the information shared in your release.

Spoon-feed reporters the raw material they need to craft a story and shape it in their own way to serve their specialized markets. That's how you can score big with a simple press release. But it's not the only way.

You can also score coverage when editors recast your release into a short article to fill space on a page. In order to reach your objective however, you need to cut through the garbage and make a big impact – FAST. That's exactly what a strong headline can do for you.

Gain a solid understanding of the magazine or radio station you plan to hit. Knowing what kind of material they typically cover is the key to delivering a message that wins.

Use press releases to announce new products or upcoming events (something that hasn't happened yet)... or to report an experience or outcome (something that has already happened) related to your product, service, or business. It's considered news when it's fresh (or freshly spun) and fits in with the existing issues and interests of those served by your target media outlet.

Appeal to human nature. Point your headline to tap into the mindset of the marketplace you're addressing. Remember that in a press release, you're targeting a specific market. You're reaching both those who *communicate* and *consume* information. Deliver news the audience would want to know about. But realize that nobody knows more about the kind of information those folks desire than a seasoned editor.

Since people in general are primarily interested in themselves and their needs and desires, that's exactly what you should hit on.

How can you tell your story in a way that benefits the editor/writer while focusing on the end consumer? When you push the right buttons, you serve editors with a timely message that catches the eye and diverts attention away from the mountain of paperwork staring them in the face. Do this and you're making their job just a little bit easier and life tends to favour those who ease the paths of others. At the same time, you've focused on what the audience cares about. So you're providing information that's in alignment and is therefore more likely to be noticed.

Give them fresh, juicy, timely, on-target information in a compelling way and you increase your odds. This approach works. It's what gets you out of the bleachers and into the game -- and that's the only way you can win.

As you set out to write your headline, think about how you can turn it into an interesting news story. Think about what you have to announce... an angle you could take... who has used it and what happened when they did... and why an editor (and readers) should care.

Discovering and presenting a news connection is vital.

Think about what makes your product, service, or company unique from anything else out there. How does this distinction BENEFIT the audience? What makes your story important? You're dealing with the media and they're trained to look for facts. Anything unsubstantiated is quickly discounted as fluff and tossed aside, as is anything that looks or suggests marketing or advertising.

Press Release Headline Tips

The best way to begin crafting a killer press release headline (far and away the most important words of the entire document) is to start with a series of lists -- facts, features, details and benefits.

Think about your dominant benefit, most unique attribute, greatest value advantage, or the single most important fact related to your product. List the things that make what you have to offer different from anything else. What aspect or angle would make it interesting to this marketplace?

Figure out a way to make your message newsworthy and inject this *news perspective* into your headline. Spin it into a news story.

What can give your message a "newsy" edge? Think about what makes it innovative, timely, original, or unusual. Give it a surprising twist to arouse curiosity and make people want to learn more about it.

Localize your headline when it fits in with your selected media. For example, if you were sending it out locally and you lived in Buffalo, NY– you could give your headline a local feel with this kind of beginning: *"Cheektowaga man _____ (insert verb here)..."* Local people will immediately identify with you and your message because you're one of them.

For ideas and inspiration, look no further than the magazine rack at the supermarket checkout. There you'll find plenty of ideas from magazines that rely on the power of *news-style headlines* gracing their covers to sell hundreds of thousands of copies on the spot. Use these headlines as triggers to stimulate your own creativity.

Take a look the next time you go shopping and you'll spot examples like these that could easily be converted into news-style headlines:

Don't Let This Cancer Sneak Up On You

Want To Live To Be 100? More and more people are living to a ripe old age. You can too.

Conquering Fear – Are we too afraid?

Bankers Who Are Loved – They partner, advise, mentor, support...

202

and by the way, even lend

Miso Medicine – Japanese Staple Inspires Warming Winter Soups

15-Minute Fat Burners – Workout Moves That Get The Job Done Fast

8 Laws of Building Wealth – The Strategies That Work Now

Press release headlines need to make an impact quickly. Say it in a dozen words or so. Less is fine too if it packs an adequate punch. There's no room for any extra baggage here. You've got to spit it out fast and make a splash to avoid being trashed.

Be specific with your news. Make it clear what is notable or remarkable about your product or story. What would make it interesting to others? Relate to the audience and make your "news" part of the bigger picture that affecting their lives.

Add a hook. Insert a surprising claim or twist. Then back it up in your body copy. Use a controversial statement that gets attention or creates curiosity. Write a headline that's connected to a current hot news story. Any of these can make your headline impossible to ignore.

Don't hold back. Make a boastful, even outrageous claim -- as long as you can support it with facts. It's the nature of reporters to challenge your claims. But if your message is built on a sturdy foundation, this can be a huge benefit to you in the end.

A strong headline will win you more of an editor's time -- at least the time required to read further and imagine how your information might be best used. A weak headline with doom your publicity efforts from the start. How far an editor reads on and what comes out of it as a result depends on your effectiveness at snagging and maintaining interest.

Make your language match the media. Choose words that correspond and connect. Make it sound like something right off the pages of that specific publication. Don't just blindly send out your releases; target them, especially with your headlines. Use words that instantly resonate with your narrowly defined audience. When you speak their language, you have a much better shot at being heard.

People in general are most interested in themselves. They're wrapped up by the issues that occupy their thoughts. They also like hearing about other interesting people. Just look at all the magazines and television shows today about "celebrities".

Take the information you have and recast it into a news story for your chosen market. Customize it to fit the media outlet.

Your success with press releases is largely dependent on the news value and relevant worth of the message communicated by your headline.

As it is with any headline, you'll find that writing several different versions helps you refine it into one that works. Eventually your efforts pay off. But it often takes a number of variations and modifications to get it just right.

Move things around. Try saying it another way. Compress or expand. And don't forget to have fun with it.

Use plain language that everyone understands and avoid showing off your extensive vocabulary. Remember, you're trying to connect with the minds and hearts of human beings and to do so means speaking clearly and simply about a key issue that's sure to be of interest.

3 key factors to writing powerful press release headlines are:

1. *News Value*

2. *Instant Impact*

3. *Timeliness of Your Message*

Editing Your Headlines To Sharpen Their Effectiveness

When crafting your news release, it's vital to avoid anything that even hints at sales or marketing hype.

Reporters are trained to ferret out the facts and can spot unsubstantiated claims a mile away. Avoid any semblance of marketing hype by deleting advertising words like breakthrough, unique, extraordinary, revolutionary, spectacular, incredible, amazing, and the like in your media communications.

No member of the media is interested in promoting your business directly -- that's what paid advertising is for. But they love to cover events and interesting developments and then repackage these as human interest *stories* their audiences will welcome and appreciate.

Be extra careful about spelling mistakes and grammatical errors. For those who work with words all day long, even the slightest gaff can be enough to send them running in the opposite direction.

Avoid irrelevant or weak headlines. If it doesn't fit and it doesn't pull, it doesn't belong. Be judicious with your headline editing because it's your one chance to penetrate the media barrier.

Reduce the number of words. Once you've whittled your headline choices down to just a few, revise to reduce word usage. What you want to do is communicate a compelling thought in as few words as possible. It shouldn't tell the full story -- just enough to woo the reporter inside. Be sure to make your headline no longer than two lines of text at the absolute maximum.

Take a look at your proposed headline. If you think it could be stronger, try revising your action word. Does a replacement verb communicate the intended thought more effectively? The best way to employ action words is in the present tense. This adds immediacy to your message, thus increasing your odds of getting noticed in a busy world.

Remove the unnecessary. Look for words that don't really add anything – words like *of, that,* or *which* and delete them. If the message is just as strong without these words, go with the leaner version.

Rewrite your headline until it's clear, concise and engaging. The words need to flow smoothly and they need to plant an engaging thought that can't be misconstrued.

Eliminate exclamation marks and any other tools of emphasis other than capitalization. Those are sure signs of a sales message. Some people prefer to set press release headlines in all UPPER CASE letters. This is one way to clearly distinguish the headline from the body of the message.

A solid choice is to capitalize only the first letter of each word. It's also a good idea to set your headline in a larger size. A 14 point to 20 point font works well here. But you'll have to adapt the size to fit your message all on one page -- a much preferred approach. Just don't make it look like advertising.

Sample Press Release Headlines

"World's Fastest Reader Offers Special Report To Help Make Reading Newspapers More Fun"
(Mike Van Norden)

"World's Fastest Reader Reveals Secrets To Being A Genius!"
(Mike Van Norden)

"New Jersey Man Really Sells The Brooklyn Bridge... For $14.95"
(Paul Hartunian)

"Do You, Your Staff, or Your Listeners Write Like Millionaires?"
(Bart Baggett)

"New Source Promises Fresh-Roasted Spice Blends & Quick-Fix Recipes To Turn Everyday Foods Into Gourmet Delights"
(Success Track)

"Book Turns Lonely Guys Into Ladies Men In One Reading"
(Arthur Gordon)

"Local Tax Expert Generates Over $1,000,000 In Tax Refunds"
(Brian Maroevich)

"72 Year Old Man Banned From Casinos After Discovering How To Beat Them At Black Jack"
(Bill Myers)

"10 Simple Things You Can Do To Protect Yourself Against Attacks While Travelling"
(Ron Ruiz)

"Low Fat Cooking That Will Make Your Mouth Water"
(Cynthia Denton)

"What Do Garth, Shania & Clint Have in Common?"
(Bart Baggett)

"Latin Lover Reveals How Any Man Can Become A Champion of Charm"
(Anthony Blake)

"How 10 Years Of Stuffing My Face Led To Internet Enterprise"
(Hollis Thomases)

"College Money Crisis Not Necessary - $135 Million Available To Students Who Know Where To Look"
(Joe Vitale)

"Creative Publicity Ideas Pay Off, Consultant Claims In New Booklet"
(Marcia Yudkin)

"Checklist With Special Report Detect and Explain Underachieving Child In School"
(Mike Van Norden)

"New Special Report Makes Online Dating Safer and 93.7% More Successful"
(Success Track)

"A Date or a Disater? How To Boost Your Chances By 93.7%"
(Success Track)

"15 Modern Marketing Masters Share Their Best Secrets – For Free"
(Bob Serling)

"19 Top Online Copywriters Teach Internet Marketers How To Turn Words Into Cash With Irresistible Sales Letters"
(Dan Lok)

"Powerball Lottery Hoax Revealed As Internet Marketing Strategy For Publicity-Seeking Author"
(Joe Vitale)

"Great For Retirees and Stay-At-Home Moms – Free Booklet On The Art Of Growing Landscape Plants For Fun and Profit"
(Mike McGroarty)

"Renegade Copywriter Releases Notes to Rarest Book Ever on Copywriting"
(Harlan Kilstein)

"New Ways To Turn Yellow Pages Into Gold"
(Success Track)

"Marketing Sells More With Copywriting Checklist"
(Mike Pavlish)

New Web Site, landrystadium.org. Offers Texans Opportunity To Cast Vote
(Mike Van Norden)

"Recent Survey Confirms That Most Computer-Reliant Small Businesses Still Don't Back-Up Critical Data Files Regularly"

"Forced To Quit High School Just Short Of Graduating As Valedictorian, Local Woman Finds Success As Internet Entrepreneur"
(Lisa Hickman Bryan)

"Herbal Remedy Treatment For Cold Sores and Genital Herpes Brings New Hope To Those Who Don't Respond To Traditional Treatment"
(Lynda Gorman)

"New Ways To Make In-Demand Crafts From Everyday Trash"

"Source Reveals 1,000 Companies That Pay You To Work At Home"
(Lee Michaels)

"Video Tape Helps Parents and Police Locate Missing Children"
(Jon Wright)

"Shoe Repair Comes to the Customer's Front Door"
(Kenneth Morgan)

"Author Picks Fight With Harry Potter – and Wins; #2 Bestseller Uses Internet in Clever New Ways To Sell Books"
(Joe Vitale)

"New Ways To Make Furniture – and More – From Scrap"
(Joe Vitale)

"The Secrets Of Staying Married And Staying Happy"

"New Guide Reveals The Best-Kept Secrets Of New York's Top Chefs"

"Move over DaVinci Code: Unknown Author's 'The Adsense Code' is #3 Bestseller on Amazon"
(Joel Comm)

"Is Your Station Manager Sexually Frustrated? Handwriting Expert Reveals The 'Truth' About Your On-Air Personalities and Staff's Sex Life"
(Mike Van Norden)

"Florida Hypnotist challenges Mayo Clinic: I can cure the yips – guaranteed"
(Harlan Kilstein)

"Is Your Organization Reaping The Benefits of a Changing Workforce?"
(Topnotch Employment Inc.)

"Leaving Secrets: How To Create A Personal Instruction Manual For Life"
(Joe Vitale)

"New Manual Teaches Aspiring Bodybuilders Safe, Natural Way To Build Strength"
(Al Alfaro)

"P.T. Barnum Expert Says 'There's a sucker born every minute' Never Spoken By The Great Circus Promoter"
(Joe Vitale)

Chapter 13

Creating Information Product
Titles/Headlines That Sell

"I think any public notice I may have had comes from titles. Nobody was more surprised than I when 'The Man Nobody Knows' became a best seller. The title is what sold the book."

Bruce Barton

How effective are your product titles?

When you begin to think of titles as headlines, they take on a whole new meaning. Like the headline at the top of an advertisement, your information product needs a powerful banner to momentarily seize the attention, interest and imagination of the specific group of people it was created for.

Why Strong Info-Product Titles Are So Important

There's no question about the power of the headline in all types of marketing communications. They reach out to the prospect, with a message of utmost importance, drawing him inside the body copy where a pre-existing interest continues to build. Without the headline, how effectively would the same ad perform? Similarly, it's the title of an article, report, book, home-study course, audio CD, or DVD training program that either attracts the right kind of attention, or sends it elsewhere.

The title is a major selling tool -- regardless of the format your information takes. In fact, your title is your strongest marketing weapon.

Imagine an entire page of book listings in a particular category. There could be hundreds, even thousands of informational pieces listed and each one is identified by its *title* alone. In other words, your info-product listing is assigned the exact amount of space as all the others. The only difference between them is the collection of words composed as titles by their respective authors. Each title is unique. *But how many of them reach out and grab the person they were written for by the collar?* Chances are in any given list of products, few have the kind of heading-like title that leaps off the page and speaks directly to the audience in a way that's impossible to ignore.

If all you had to market your goods was the title, would your choice of words do an adequate selling job?

People do judge based on first impressions. If they can see your product, or an image of it, they often make a snap assessment. Invariably the turning point and deciding factor is the title. Your title determines relevancy and significance. It makes all the difference in terms of seizing the time and attention of those who see it.

No one looks at the interior first. It just doesn't happen that way.

The only way they get beyond the title and cover is when what they've already observed sends a positive signal. It's a green light that encourages a continuation to discover more information from the product itself, customer reviews, or sales copy.

When you hit the *hot button* of your intended target with your title, it generates an instant and positive reaction. You've captured their interest and drawn them inside. Conversely, a title that misses the mark is overlooked or ignored.

Titles set the stage. Every title or headline is the *"ticket on the meat"* as advertising legend, David Ogilvy once described it. Titles trigger an instant and often subconscious response and like opposite ends of a magnet, it either pulls or pushes away those who process the message contained.

Most of us are preoccupied much of the time. It's a condition of modern society, so we've adapted our behaviour in ways that allow us to filter out multiple distractions from a variety of sources.

As humans, we tend to go through life with our minds only half turned on and proceed in this trance-like state looking for promising clues that could lead us to a desired result.

Though the overwhelming majority of these messages are ignored, those in tune with our thoughts get through. They gain filter-free access to our minds because they speak to us as emotional beings. Anything near and dear to our hearts cuts through the clutter. It's something we automatically pay attention to. As we set out in search of specific information, the parameters have been set. Now it's a matter of sifting through a mass of titles, looking for the most relevant and appealing ones.

Your title needs to hit hard and fast. You've got to stop prospects cold as they actively search and redirect their focus from multiple listings to your specific information.

If you want to get your piece into the hands of more people, give your title a lift. Make it more arresting... more targeted... more alluring. The format doesn't matter. Information of all kinds -- from the smallest articles and blog posts to the largest multimedia courses -- can be much more effective with a compelling title.

First impressions count. People do judge books and other informational pieces by their covers and even more specifically -- by the titles presented on those covers. As self-publishing expert, Dan Poynter says, *"The package outside sells the product inside."*

What Kind Of Titles Work Best?

Your best title format often depends on the product and your objectives. Decide what you're going to create before considering title options.

If it's an article, a one-line teaser like the kind on the covers of magazines like National Enquirer, Cosmopolitan and Men's Health. These titles are clear, concise and crisp. They tempt, tease and tantalize readers – selling hundreds of thousands of copies every month to people waiting in line to pay for their groceries.

Below, you'll find several examples. Some of these titles could be used as is, while others would require some reworking if they were to be used as product titles.

National Enquirer

Plastic Surgery Shockers – Nip, Tuck, and Yuck!
Meanest Mom in America – You Won't Believe What She Did!

Best and Worst Celebrity Diets – Who Gained and Lost The Most

Cosmopolitan

The #1 Secret of Confident Chicks
One Question No Guy Can Resist
Jilted At The Altar – How It Feels To Be Dumped Before Your Wedding
Day

Men's Health

10 Greatest Ab Exercises Ever!
Amazing New Heart-Disease Breakthrough
Instant Sex – Touch Her Right Here

Woman's Health

Success Without Distress - Discover a Happier, Healthier You
More Energy – Instantly
Lose Your Belly! Weight Loss Secrets That Work

Money

How To Thrive In A Bad Economy
6 Ways To Bulletproof Your Job
The 15 Best Investments For Income Now

CondeNast Traveller

Best Islands! 37 Easy Escapes
India's Secret Paradise
Ultimate Greek Island Finder - 20 Top Isles For Beaches, Beauty, Hotels
and More

Below are information product titles from master copywriter/self-publisher, Gary Halbert. Each one was conceived as a special report title.

- How To Flatten Your Stomach In The Fastest Way Humanly Possible

- What To Do About Arthritis Pain

- How To Pick Up Girls Instantly – Anywhere In The World

- How To Get What The U.S. Government Owes You

- 27 Secret Ways To Melt Off Body Fat – Hour By Hour

- How To Negotiate and Win No Matter Who You're Up Against

- Latest Facts On How To Cure Prostate Problems

- 57 Proven Ways To Lower Your Golf Score

- How To Make A Fortune In The Coming Real Estate Bloodbath

- How To Protect Your Family and Wealth As "Nouveau Riche" Mobsters Infiltrate New (and Formerly Legitimate) Businesses By The Hundreds

If it's a book title (non-fiction) you're working on to sell through traditional bookstores and online, use a title/subtitle combination. In this case the title serves as the identifying name, while the subtitle delivers the punch. In any event, your title in its totality should nail the subject in a powerful and provocative way.

Here are some (mostly recent) examples of title/subtitle combinations:

How To Become An Entrepreneurial Genius: *Your Blueprint To More Money, More Respect and More Freedom* (Ron Chenier)

Happy For No Reason – *7 Steps To Being Happy From The Inside Out* (Marci Shimoff)

The 4-Hour Workweek – *Escape 9-5, Live Anywhere, and Join The New Rich* (Timothy Ferriss)

Zero Limits – *The Secret Hawaiian System for Wealth, Health, Peace and More* (Joe Vitale)

A Complaint-Free World – *How to Stop Complaining and Start Enjoying the Life You Always Wanted* (Will Bowen)

How To Talk To Anybody About Anything – *Breaking The Ice With Everyone From Accountants To Zen Buddhists* (Leil Lowndes)

Fishing Secrets – *101 Ways To Improve Your Fishing* (Jerome K.

Knap)

Mindmapping – *Your Personal Guide To Exploring Creativity and Problem-Solving* (Joyce Wycoff)

Fat-Fighting Foods – *Low-Fat Foods For A Healthier You* (Susan Male Smith & Denise Webb)

Age of Propaganda – *The Everyday Use and Abuse of Persuasion* (Anthony Pratkanis & Elliot Aronson)

The Power of Superfoods – *30 Days That Will Change Your Life* (Sam Graci)

How To Give A Damn Good Speech – *Even When You Have No Time To Prepare* (Philip R. Theibert)

Notice how many of these subtitles have headline appeal. *"How to Stop Complaining and Start Enjoying the Life You Always Wanted"*... *"101 Ways To Improve Your Fishing"*... and *"30 Days That Will Change Your Life"* all deliver specific benefits in an enticing way.

You can triple the power of a subtitle by declaring 3 specific and enticing advantages offered within the product's content. Here's how Jerry Fisher pulled it off in fine fashion:

Title: Creating Successful Small Business Advertising
Subtitle: *How to develop the headline that stops them, the message that sells them and the look that sets you apart*

Use whatever format suits your particular application. Just be sure your title accomplishes the following two important tasks. Your title needs to...

1. Capture the immediate interest of your target audience

2. Generate feelings of excitement, enthusiasm and anticipation for more of the same

When you give your audience what they want to hear, you'll attract larger numbers.

Invariably, the magical pull of information lies not in the product itself -- but in what that product does for the buyer, end user, or consumer.

It's not the paper... the CD's... or DVDs... and it's not even the actual information contained in the product itself. Instead, what makes your title work is the anticipated BENEFIT they get out your information. That's what counts. Audiences are out there waiting for that *big promise*. It's the one magical answer to their particular problem, or the one thing that will advance them in the direction they want to go. Hit on it and your title has a magnetic pull.

The message communicated FIRST needs to fit your target audience. Don't leave them guessing -- they won't. Instead, the vast majority will simply move on.

If your information covers tax-saving tips for people who work from home – be sure to say so somewhere in your title. For example... *"101 Timely Tax-Saving Secrets for Home-Based Entrepreneurs"*. If you just use *"101 Timely Tax-Saving Tips"* -- it's not clear who you're speaking to. So your title wouldn't have the same powers of attraction in the specific market you're trying to reach. Make your title message fit the target and those within that group will be drawn to it -- naturally and automatically.

Using an original concept in your title can make it memorable. When people can remember the name of your product, it's easy to tell others about it.

Below are some examples of books that express original concepts in their names. It's important to note that some of these names, though memorable, lack a strong benefit within the main title. But they do however, deliver the payoff in the subtitle.

Blue Ocean Strategy – *How To Create Uncontested Market Space and Make The Competition Irrelevant* (W. Chad Kim & Renee Mauborgne)

Good To Great – *Why Some Companies Make The Leap... and Others Don't* (Jim Collins)

The Tipping Point – *How Little Things Can Make A Big Difference* (Malcolm Gladwell)

The Big Red Fez – *How To Make Any Website Better* (Seth Godin)

The Wellness Revolution – *How To Make A Fortune In The Next*

Trillion Dollar Industry (Paul Zane Pilzer)

The Mega Strategy – *The Exciting New Million-Dollar Home Business Enterprise That Anyone Can Launch Successfully With Minimal Investment or Risk* (Dan Lee Dimke)

You could also deliver a straightforward title that conveys clearly and interestingly what your information product reveals. With this approach, teaching the reader "How To" do something of interest is a proven path to success (*refer to the examples from Gary Halbert*).

Think about how the information you have to share serves the reader directly. Then all you have to do is state it in an interesting or intriguing way to hook your audience.

Effective information product titles often promise the following:

- How to complete a specific task

- How to learn a new skill

- How to improve life in some way

- How to solve a problem

- How to do something faster or easier

- How to make money in a specific way

- How to attain a desired result the easy way

If you want your title to attract maximum interest from those you intend to reach, you've got to nail the subject matter in the headline. That's the key. If it's unclear what subject you cover, you cannot expect anyone to investigate further. There are multiple options available, so you've got to deliver your product's message succinctly and enticingly.

Make your product's most unique characteristic shine through. What's different about your methods? People are hungry for new and different information.

Address the dominant hunger your product satisfies and your results can be instant and automatic. Find out what they're already buying and position your title in a way that satisfies the hunger. Obviously your content must be in alignment. But knowing what issues are most in demand and that have active buyers can set you up for success when your title makes an instant and powerful connection.

3 Things Your Title Should Do

1. Attract Interested Eyeballs

In order to maximize the return on your creative efforts, you need to capture the right kind of interest. This means that your title needs to command the attention and fuel the interest of those within your niche.

Put your proposed title to the test. Is it likely to appeal to your targeted group? You want a title that reads like a headline. You want something that jumps right out and grabs your reader's interest, seizes their imagination and creates an intense emotional desire for more.

2. Deliver Your Ultimate Benefit

What is the cumulative effect of every morsel of information you share? That's your *ultimate benefit*. It's the much-sought answer to a challenge, or the solution to a problem. Not only do you have what the prospect wants, but when you can communicate it in such a way that it speaks to both the mind and the heart, you are in essence presenting a *magic pill*. It's the easy answer to their frustrations and disappointments. It's exactly what they wanted... and now it's within reach. Strike a nerve and you often strike gold.

3. Convey The Essence of Your Idea Instantly

Come out swinging with your best punch. Deliver your core information with power, precision and promise. Tell them on the outside of the package what they can expect on the inside. But do it fast.

Think of your title as an independent entity. It's got to be strong enough to generate interest and immediate action. Make it stand out. Make it memorable enough so it's easy for people to recommend to others. And make your title figuratively leap off the page and trigger a "must read" reaction.

Optional Add-Ons

Below are three extra elements you could work into your info-product titles for added effect.

1. Incorporate Your Own Brand

If you've got a series of related reports, books, interviews, audio presentations – whatever – it's a good idea to create a distinct brand name you can add to all your titles. Think about the *"Dummies"* brand of books with hundreds of different topics covered, all essentially following the same format. Whenever most people hear about a *"Dummies"* title, they know exactly what to expect. That's branding at work.

The *"Complete Idiot's Guide"* line of books is another well-known example of a branded group of products. *"The Truth About"* series of short books on various topics related to body, mind and spirit also uses this idea effectively.

If you're planning more of a similar type of product, identify your brand in each title and you'll gain recognition faster, while generating, additional and automatic sales down the line.

2. Keywords Targeted To Your Audience

Keywords help widen your net by capturing the attention of a wider audience. For example, *"Sneakiest Uses for Everyday Things: How to Make a Boomerang with a Business Card, Convert a Pencil into a Microphone, Make Animated Origami, Turn a TV ... Create Alternative Energy Science Projects"* is a title that delivers abundant information. But if the author used only *"Sneakiest Uses for Everyday Things"*, would it have been as effective? Sure, he might have attracted more viewers of a general nature. But my guess is that the shorter title would likely deliver fewer buyers. Add specific keywords prospects can relate to and it's as though you're calling out to them by name.

Let's take a look at another example: *"Making Divorce Easier on Your Child: 50 Effective Ways to Help Children Adjust"*. Here, the main title conveys the essence of the author's message quite well. But adding the keyword phrase *"Help Children Adjust"* adds an extra line in the water

– one that's sure to hook those with this particular thought in mind.

The same could be said for this title: "*101 Ways to Market Your Online Jewelry Shop: Free and Cheap Ways to Market, Promote, Advertise, and Increase Traffic to Your Online or Etsy Jewelry Shop and Sell Your Jewelry Now*". Lots of extra keywords added serves those browsing as well as anyone entering these keywords into any search engine field. Pack your title with keywords and you'll attract more of the right kind of people.

3. **Popular Title Words and Phrases**

Another option is to use the tried and true "template" words in your product titles. These can work in headlines and information product titles.

Here are some of the more popular title words and phrases:

- How To...
- 101 Ways To...
- Secrets Of...
- New...
- Fast...
- Quick...
- Quick and Easy...
- Easy Ways To...·
- ... Method
- ... System
- ... For Fun and Profit
- The Lazy Way To...

100 Million Books Sold Using Nothing But Titles

Back in the 1920's, E. Haldeman Julius built a publishing empire based on his "Little Blue Books" -- a series of short, booklet-style publications on numerous topics. More than 100 million copies were sold through simple display ads in newspapers and magazines across the country. Many years later, Julius shared his discoveries in the book, *The First Hundred Million.*

Each *Little Blue Book* offered cost just five cents. But buyers had to make 20 selections with each order and they could choose whatever books they wanted from the many listed in the ad.

What was particularly interesting about this venture was that each advertisement listed nothing but the titles of the numerous books available. No ad copy was included. *Each volume had to sell based on the title alone.* If any booklet didn't sell 10,000 copies in the previous year, it was revised and the new title replaced the original in subsequent advertisements.

As an example, the booklet called *"Patent Medicine"* sold 3000 copies. When the title was changed to *"The Truth About Patent Medicine"* -- sales increased to about 10,000 units.

"How To" was another title template that worked well back then, just as it does today. *"Psycho-Analysis Explained"* sold approximately 5,000 copies. *"How To Psycho-Analyze Yourself"* sold 43,000 -- a huge improvement.

What Julius discovered was that the best results occurred when these winning words and phrases were included:

- The Truth About...
- How To...
- Facts You Should Know...
- ... Made Simple
- ... Made Plain
- Life...
- Love...
- Hints On...

Now let's suppose you owned a health food store. As an alternative health enthusiast, you decided to write a series of reports and offer them for sale in the book isle of your shop. You could use what you just learned from E. Haldeman Julius to create captivating titles like...

The Facts You Should Know About The Flu Shot
The Truth About Nature's Pharmacy Your Doctor Never Told You
How To Reverse The Aging Process With Natural Herbs

The trick is to hit the *bullseye* of your target market. This means cutting through the barrage of messages with a direct hit. *Wham!* -- your title or headline hits with full force and triggers an instant emotional reaction without requiring any thinking.

How effectively and appealingly your title states what it's all about can make a huge difference. Tap into their existing mindset with a solution that so far has remained unresolved. Sizzling, headline-like titles instantly captivate audiences.

Think about it this way: you want everything you write to be consumed rather than bypassed. But it's a constant battle for the sustained attention of your reader. Therefore, the frequent use of attention-grabbing titles and subtitles strengthens your material because you continue to reach out and pull them inside.

Applying what you've learned about headlines to your titles, subtitles and chapter titles will definitely make them more interesting and alluring. Whatever you're writing, add interesting headlines as you go and you'll compel readers to stick around for more. Keep them engaged and your efforts will pay off to a greater degree.

A compelling title pulls like a powerful magnet. But a weak title, or having no title at all means you're not using your biggest gun to create anticipation, interest and enthusiasm.

How To Craft A Powerful Title

When you set out to create a title, begin by brainstorming all the things your "inside" information will do for people. What makes your information more valuable or unique? Does it help others do something better, faster, easier, or cheaper? What is the one breakthrough idea revealed inside?

That's what you want to hint at in your title.

Saturate your mind with facts, insights and all the advantages of your information. Then forget about it completely. Let your subconscious mind go to work on the puzzle while you do something else for the rest of the day. Don't give any more conscious effort to creating a blockbuster title. Instead, pay attention to the nuggets revealed by your inner mind. As you're made aware of these, quickly write them down. That's the only way to prevent your best ideas from floating away and being forgotten.

Build a list and then experiment with several template title ideas. For example... *"7 Ways To..."* might be an appropriate start to a title for an article or report. Test several of these "plug 'n play" solutions. Change the words to make it a better fit or a stronger one.

If you've narrowed it down to a few solid contenders and you can't quite decide on your own, poll your customers, visitors, or subscribers and ask which product they would most prefer. Conversely, write an article and then place your possible titles on your home page and monitor which one gets clicked the most. This kind of test can be helpful because the decision is made by those you intend to serve.

Key Title Components

Whenever you plan on creating an effective title for any information product, consider the following significant factors.

An effective title should reveal:

1. The specific topic or subject matter revealed in the content

2. Who specifically the content is written for

3. A big promise, or the ultimate advantage or benefit

You want to make your title stand out and the best way to do that is through the core advantage, value, uniqueness, and newsworthiness of your information.

It's important to communicate with clarity. Speak directly to your audience of one -- in a way they can't miss. In fact, you want them to instantly recognize that your words are exactly what they need. State it concisely (up to 7 words for a main title) and precisely so your words trigger an instantaneous and powerful pull and a thundering "that's for me!" gut-level reaction.

Those in your target market are going about the daily routines of their lives. In the back of their minds, there's a persistent nudge that just won't go away. Suddenly they happen upon your riveting title. It's exactly what they want. They want to fulfill the promise conveyed on the label.

Your title suggests the answer they've long sought to resolve an issue that's only been suppressed -- until now. What you have to offer is news to them. It's something your audience hasn't seen before.

Terrific titles don't merely reveal their subject, but convey a sense of discovery not previously available. They arouse curiosity... command attention... and momentarily seize the imagination of the intended reader.

When you make the right connection with your audience -- the mere act of ordering, downloading, bookmarking, etc., creates an instant feeling of euphoria. Subconsciously, there's an "Aha – that's it!" feeling that permeates and the actual act of making a purchase or saving the material feels fabulous because in their minds, the problem is as good as solved.

Whatever title you ultimately choose should generate interest and stimulate the imagination of others. If you're selling directly, you need only focus on the consumer. But if you're selling information through distributors and stores, use a title that conveys a powerful idea -- one that creates improvement in some area. Or, one they can get enthusiastic about promoting. Make your title appear as a much-wanted solution, or the ultimate "fix" for those frustrated by the other options they know about.

A promising, benefit-oriented title is usually more effective than a cool or funny one. Clever, catchy, or funny titles can be more memorable and that's not a bad attribute to have working in your favour. However, if your information is for sale, you need to assess the selling power of such an approach.

A strong benefit-laden title that generates lots of interest is usually the safest route to take.

If the only selling tool you have is your title, the question to ask is

-- does your selection work? Does your headline alone make people excited about reading on to get more details? If not, keep working on it.

Weak titles fail to draw audiences and leave a bad first impression. Yours needs to reach out with a message of promise and possibility. Strike a nerve and you'll turn heads and grab hearts.

Titles and Subtitles

You'll find that most main titles of books are short and sweet. Some are just a single word that provides little description of the content below the surface. That's where an effective subhead steps in to fill the void. If the only information given about Malcolm Gladwell's book was the main title, *"The Tipping Point"* -- few would know what it was about without digging in. But add the subtitle -- *"How Little Things Can Make a Big Difference"* and the pieces of the puzzle begin to fall into place.

Subtitles add detail and substance. They pack more punch into main headings and titles. Subtitles also make it easy to offer customized versions of an information product to serve specialized markets.

Short titles are more memorable, making your product a more likely beneficiary of word-of-mouth marketing. But it's the subtitle that often delivers the key essentials about the content contained within.

Spend some time and creative energy evolving your title and subtitle on major products. But even a short article can be made exponentially more effective and be seen by a lot more people by assigning a title that automatically generates interest. Improved titles increase exposure, generate greater interest and boost sales.

"A good title is a work of genius." -- E. Haldeman Julius

Chapter 14

A Brief Word About Some Additional Headline Applications

Sales Letters

Sales letter headlines can be very long or fairly short. In sales letters, headlines are not limited by a lack of space. Whenever appropriate, take advantage of options like super-headlines and subheads to accentuate your main headline. These options simply aren't practical for most other uses, so use them on your longer letters.

Sales letters also allow for a wide array of design options. Take full advantage of large type sizes, bold type, text boxes, and other choices that fit your message. Remember however, to use these tools with a reasonable degree of restraint.

In some cases it may even be preferable to not use a traditional headline in a sales letter. This may be the case when you want to create a more personal, one-on-one communication. When you do this, most of the principles of creating attention-getting, interest-arousing headlines, actually apply to your opening lines of text. You still have to work just as hard to gain and sustain your prospects interest.

"How To Increase Your Profits In An Economic Climate" (Peter Sun)

"How To Get Your Athletes To Perform Their Absolute BEST When Everything Depends On It: The 7 Secrets That Can Make You A Winning Coach" (Carl Galletti)

"How To End Worries Over Scraggly Lawns" (Robert Collier)

"Whoever Said There's No Such Thing As A Free Lunch Didn't Know About This Letter." (Murray Raphel)

"Now The Far Distances Are Yours WITH MAGIC EYES THAT

SEE FOR MILES!" (Robert Collier)

"My simple, proven, step-by-step formula will show you:

How To Get All The Hot Leads and Customers You'll Ever Need For Your Business… 100% Guaranteed!

And no… I'm not going to charge you my normal $12,500 fee! Instead, I've created an incredible course that's jam-packed with every last one of my most closely guarded secrets, and I'm going to virtually give it away to you for peanuts." (Brian Keith Voiles)

"How To Make Big Money Writing And Selling Booklets In The Next 30 Days" (Steve Manning)

"How To Turn Your Info-Product Into Instant Cash!"

"Thousands are already profiting from this proven money-making system. Now it's your turn to…

Make More Money In A Few Hours Than Most People Earn All Week!

If you're searching for a surefire way to make an extra $1,000 - $5,000 every week, for the rest of your life… this information may be more important to your financial future than anything you've ever read…"

"Deeply in debt and worried about survival, I discovered…

"The Secret To Becoming A Millionaire Is Simply Using The Right Words!"

You are 17 words or less away from a fortune! I'll reveal all the 'magic' words you'll ever need in my new book. Picture yourself earning several hundred thousand dollars a year. Work a few hours from the comfort of home, at a leisurely pace." (Ted Nicholas)

Display Ads

One common characteristic of display ad headlines is their

tendency to be extremely short and to the point. With many display ads, particularly the smaller ones, the headline needs to work even harder to arrest the attention of prospects.

To achieve visual prominence, try employing unusually large-sized text -- one quarter to one half the size of the entire ad. That doesn't mean that the entire headline has to be limited to a few short words. You could use a much longer headline and achieve the same effect by focusing on a key word or phrase, and then increasing the size of it by a huge margin so just this segment of the headline jumps out from the ad.

SPARE TIME CASH!

BUY NO DESK… Until You've Seen The Sensation Of The Business Show

THINK SMALL (Volkswagen)

"AAAHH" (Jerry Fisher)

How Will You Look After Cosmetic Surgery? (Jerry Fisher)

Online Investment Secrets!

FREE Home Alarm Installations!

Postcards

With postcards, you face a formidable task: getting noticed in a sea of other mail that has the look of more important correspondence. So you need to hit fast and you need to hit hard. Refine, revise and reduce your most compelling headline down to a handful of words that deliver the highest potential payoff to your target market.

Use the front of the card (the side that carries the mailing address) to pique the interest of your target recipient. Try a question headline to arouse curiosity and involve prospects. A good headline that captures attention, helps to improve the likelihood that the prospect will at least take one more step and flip the card over to find out more. *That's the real power of postcards -- they only require a quick flip of the wrist for recipients to get the full impact of your message.* Follow up on the other side of the card with another engaging headline that builds on the interest already generated.

"Your Windows At 616 May Be In Need Of Replacement. Here's 5 Reasons To Call Us First For A FREE, No-Obligation Consultation..."

"FREE Recorded Message Reveals An Amazing Secret That Lets You Buy Los Angeles Real Estate Without Paying High Interest Rates Or A Big Down Payment! Call: 1-999-123-4567 Anytime, 24-Hours A Day!" (Gary Halbert)

"Your One-Stop Shop For Fast, Affordable, Professional Restorations"

"Why Put Up With Old, Money-Guzzling Windows... When You Could Be Saving Money And Enjoying The Beauty, Comfort, And Style Of Our Superior Quality Windows, NOW?"

"Why Lug Heavy Groceries Home By Yourself When You Could Have All Your Favorites Delivered To Your Door?"

Door Hangers

Here, personalization is the key. It's about creating a message that has the appearance of greater importance to the recipient. What happens when you return home and find a notice attached to your door or mailbox -- a notice from the post office or courier service? You pay attention to it immediately, don't you?

This type of message gets noticed for two reasons:

1. It's usually dropped in an uncommon location – a Post-It note on a door... a card stuck in the door frame... or a tag fastened to the door handle.

2. It's personalized – usually with your name and address.

Do the same with a door hanger and your message will get noticed. Add an element of personalization to your headline, to let the recipient know instantly that the message is for him.

"The Driveway At 616 West Blvd. Is In Need Of Repair. Get Your FREE ESTIMATE From The Paving Experts At: 111-111-1111"

"Attention Fairport Beach Residents… Here's Your Complimentary Pass To Our First Birthday Party -- Join Us At Smash Hit Videos For Free Pizza, Soft Drinks, and Balloons For The Kids!"

"FREE WATER ANALYSIS By The Water Doctor. Is Your Drinking Water Completely Safe? Take Our FREE Professional Analysis To Find Out For Sure."

Classified Ads

With classifieds, your space is squeezed to the maximum, so you have to be really selective about the words you choose for your ad.

It's best to begin with a complete statement, and then pare it down to the most concise communication possible. Place your most strongerst, most effective keywords towards the beginning of your classified.

One approach is to select your audience as a lead-in to your headline. "*Attention Diving Enthusiasts*!" By identifying your intended audience, you magnify the value of your message for those folks only, and help turn away everyone else who isn't really a prospect.

"Financial Expert Reveals Wealth-Building Secrets Any Graduate Could Use To Create A Worry-Free Future!"
"Tradesman's Inside Secrets To Professional Home Improvements."

"Last Month I Earned $4,657.38 Working Just 18 Extra Hours Per Week. I'll Show You How To Do The Same -- or Better!"

"ATTENTION CLASSIFIED ADVERTISERS! Claim Your FREE COPY of *101 Secret Ways To Turn Your Tiny Ad Into A Non-Stop, Money-Making Marketing Tool!*"

Brochures

Prospects are enticed to open and read brochures the same way they're enticed into a book. What triggers this reaction is the message conveyed on the cover. With the help of an intriguing headline and possibly a succinct subhead, you can lure interested prospects to take a peek inside your brochure.

Once you've got them on the inside -- don't let them go. The best way to prevent an instant defection is to pepper the inside of your brochure with a series of subheads or bullet points (another form of headline) to help sustain their interest.

With any brochure, spend the majority of your time developing your cover headline and subheadings. It's the most important factor in capturing targeted prospects with your brochure.

"How To Turn $40 Into $500,000 In 15 Years Or Less!"

"Enjoy A Beautiful, Healthy, Lush Lawn All Season Long… 100% Guaranteed!"

"There Are 3 Secrets To Direct Mail Success. (And you already know 2 of them.) See Inside…" (Jerry Fisher)

"Enjoy A Fresher, Cleaner, And Healthier Indoor Environment The Easy Way. Details Inside!

Envelopes

The major function of your envelope headline is to encourage the prospect to open the package and check out the contents. That's it. That's all an envelope headline or "teaser" copy needs to do.

The way to achieve this is to only mail to the best-qualified lists and just give recipients enough information to pique their interest or arouse their curiosity. Be prepared to spend plenty of time crafting your envelope headline to get it right. But it's worth the effort since direct mail envelopes are of crucial importance. The headline on the outside is your first and often *only* chance to attract interested prospects inside.

"Can You Spot The Five Mistakes Here That Make You Work More And Enjoy Your Garden Less?" (Organic Gardening)

"Let Me Write Your Problem Letters… So You Don't Have To." (Jerry Fisher)

"A Special Invitation To A Woman Who Has Reached The Interesting Age" (Lear's Magazine)

"Do You Close The Bathroom Door Even When You're The Only One Home?" (Psychology Today Magazine)

Direct Mail Packages

With most direct mail packages, the opportunities for headline applications appear with each individual part of the mailing. Typically, a direct mail package consists of an envelope, sales letter, order form, brochure ,or other enclosure and a "lift" letter. Other components may or may not be included. But each and every piece of the package can benefit from a strong headline of its own.

Here's an example of a direct mail package received from *Rodale Press*. Note the variations on the same theme used in the headlines.

Envelope: "Miracle Medicines You Can Make For Yourself In Just Minutes!"

Sales Letter: "Doctors Break Out In Cheers! … Tames Illness With A Single Dose, And Causes No Side Effects – Page 65 Great For Things That Doctors Can't Do Much About! Page 60 Will Heal You Faster Than You Can Shed Your Business Clothes After Work – Page 72"

Order Form: Try These Miracle Medicines For Yourself – FREE FOR 21 DAYS! (Absolutely No Purchase Necessary!)

Enclosure #1: "Where Ordinary Medicine Fails, These Miracle Natural Healers Can Work For You!"

Enclosure #2: "30 Days To A Low-Fat Life --YOURS FREE Just

For Previewing New Choices In Natural Healing!"

Enclosure #3: Now, All The World Is Your Healer! From Every Corner Of The Globe – Strange, Wonderful, Natural Healers That Could Keep You Out Of The Doctor's Office!

Yellow Pages Advertising

You'll be miles ahead of most Yellow Pages advertisers by simply running any type of *headline* at the top of an ad -- instead of your company name and/or logo.

Open any Yellow Pages directory from any city and you'll see what I mean; page after page of expensive display ads with names in place of headlines. This is a terrible waste of the most valuable space of any ad; the headline area. Not even the best-known brands like Coca-Cola or IBM can match the performance of a benefit-oriented headline.

Think in terms of benefits. Consider your most unique and highly desirable benefit. Condense it or select a few key words to feature in larger type. Segments of testimonials can work well for this purpose.

Another way to create a great Yellow Pages headline is to focus on your USP -- your Unique Selling Advantage or Unique Competitive Advantage. This is particularly advantageous in highly competitive categories and the right USP-based headline can make your message stand out like a bright beacon on a dark and stormy night.

"Moving Made Easier®" (UHAUL)

"We Put The Care In Home Health Care." (Para-Med)

"Your One-Stop Shop To Get Fit!" (Musclemag International)

"The Specialist In Financial Staffing" (Accountemps)

"Successful Art And Fashion Careers Begin Here" (Art Institute)

"Five Comforting Reasons You'll Be Glad You Selected ACTION+ BAIL BONDS!" (Jerry Fisher)

Fax Broadcasts

Since fax broadcasting is often seen as intrusive, your safest strategy is to offer a worthwhile payoff -- preferably a free gift of some kind -- that's sure to be appreciated. Unsolicited faxes rate right up there with unsolicited email in terms of the most despised of commercial messages. You face a huge challenge here. The objective is to get your fax to be perceived as a welcome guest, rather than another annoyance.

The best way to break through the wall of resistance is to offer something free, without obligation. Most marketers do the opposite and start flogging products right away. Don't do this. Never try to sell directly on your first contact. Build up a list of interested prospects first. Try to disarm your prospects, dissolve their natural instincts to react negatively to receiving another sales message.

Take the "sell" out of it. Give something instead, present a quick survey and provide a gift for returning it in completed form. By doing this, you'll immediately separate your efforts from the other 99% of marketers who push for the sale -- and tick people off in the process.

Another technique smart restaurant operations use, is to fax out the daily specials to area businesses. A computer hardware reseller used this same technique to provide prospects with a weekly list of new products, presented in a menu-like style. For recipients, this is perceived as a helpful service more than an advertisement.

Get right to it in your headline with *valuable news and updates* and recipients will more likely see your communication as a welcome guest instead of an intruder.

"Free Ad Evaluator Helps YOU Predict Your Success Before YOU Spend A Dime."

"Weekly Specials On Top Quality, Slightly-Used Computers, Printers, Scanners and Digital Cameras"

"We'd Like To Send You A FREE Portfolio Filled With Samples And Ideas On How You Can Increase The Value Of Your Marketing Material."

"Experience Nature Indoors… And Make Your Office A Healthier, More Productive Place To Work. FREE TRIAL!"

Catalogs

Catalog headlines work best when they focus on the important benefits of an individual item or category. Covers can focus on the value a company offers, or it can feature a number of individual items that are detailed inside.

"Our Shoes Are Crafted Of Superior Leather For Greater Comfort, Breathability And Durable Looks."

"The World's Most Flexible Clothing System For The World's Most Changeable Climate."

"Unlike Other Premium Jeans, You're Not Paying Extra For Our Name."

"How To Sell Your Home Faster And For The Highest Possible Price."

"Instant Emotional Healing… Heal Anxiety, Stress, Grief and More in Just Minutes – with the New Energy Therapies" (Learning Annex)

Business Cards, Letterhead and Advertising Specialties

Primarily, these items are seen as mediums for exchanging contact information. To that end, they do the job quite well. But if you want to make the most of these standard business tools, try adding a compelling headline -- one that reaches out to new prospects and compels them to further action. That action can be anything -- a visit to your store or showroom, a catalog request, a special premium… any one of a hundred things.

A slogan is not a headline. Most slogans would miss the mark by a wide margin in terms of attracting attention and interest. Why not replace those cute phrases with something of compelling interest to your customers and prospects? Mention your strongest benefit. Offer up your

Unique Selling Advantage. Make it very clear to recipients what's in it for them. Never assume that your prospects will figure this information out for themselves. Be clear about all you have to offer and use every available tool to communicate your message.

Following are examples of headlines that could work for business cards, or other handouts designed to serve as prospecting tools:

"Congratulations! You've just won a great prize if you see a number in this space! 49212 Call me right away. Tell me your prize-winning number. I'll tell you about the great prize you just won and send it out to you right away!" *(as seen on the back of a business card from author, copy writer, and speaker, Steve Manning)*

"FREE Checkup On Any Power Tool Or Appliance At The Tool Doctor"

"Next Day Delivery -- GUARANTEED On All Screws, Bolts, Nuts, Washers, Plugs And Anchors!"

"Call Me Today For A Free DVD -- Small Business Marketing Secrets"

"I Can Make You Famous Within 90 Days!" (bestselling author Joe Vitale)

Newsletters

Newsletters are most effective when their covers show a number of interesting headlines that relate to the theme of the publication. Newsletters are meant to be compact and informative so the first page should reveal the gist of the articles covered in detail inside. The best hard-copy newsletters feature multiple, short articles and segments. The more compelling the headlines, the more recipients want to go inside to discover additional information.

A sample issue with lots of powerful headlines makes an excellent addition to a direct mail solicitation for subscribers, or as a supplement to a press release.

With electronically dispensed newsletters (ezines), headlines should appear as close to the top of the page as possible -- and preferably within the first window that appears on the viewer's monitor.

Here are some examples of headlines featured on the front page of a small business newsletter:

"Welcome To The Best Year Of Your Life!"

"The Value Of Training In Tough Times"

"Time Management Tip -- Join The 2% Club"

"How To Write Attention-Grabbing Headlines!"

"How To Win At Telephone Tag"

"Top Goal Setting Excuses And More…"

Articles

The title of an article plays a significant role in the number of readers it attracts. Magazine publishers are well aware of this fact. Any publication that relies on newsstand sales, must feature attention-grabbing headlines that scream out to prospects and encourage them to pick up an issue.

Any article that features a riveting headline stands a far greater chance of capturing an audience, regardless of the venue -- print or online. Most print publications feature short headlines -- usually 7 words or less.

If you want to gain a quick insight into how to write compelling headlines, visit your local bookstore and peruse the magazine displays. Most major consumer publications like *Reader's Digest, Cosmopolitan, Men's Health, Prevention, Good Housekeeping, Popular Science, Vanity Fair* and other similar titles, demonstrate the science of headline writing with every issue.

Here's a list of published article titles (headlines) from recent magazine covers that demonstrate both power and brevity:

"100 Herbal Cures That Work!"

"Boost ENERGY Instantly!"

"Lose Weight NOW!"

"Great Sex Tonight!"

"Rich Desserts That Save Your Life"

"Herbs That Fight Fat!"

"What Makes Us Attractive?"

"Best Weapons Against Cancer"

"Fat-Burning Diets, Mega-Health Foods"

"The Real Power Of Vitamins"

"New Facts Women Need To Know About Their Hearts"

"How To Talk To Your Teens"

"Finesse Your Finances"

"Get Great Deals Every Time!"

"Workout 30 Minutes… Burn Fat All Day"

"Unlimited Energy -- 10 Ways To Turn It On"

"Be Better Than Her Last Lover"

"59 Fast And Healthy Dinners"

"Not Enough Sex? (We'll Fix That)"

"The Easy Way To A Flat Stomach"

"A Strong Heart In 6 Weeks"

Banner Ads

Banner ads are like small billboards that link back to the site they promote. With banners, you have an opportunity to add design techniques, color and style to your headline message. But you're better off to limit those choices to those that keep the overall file size to a minimum, thus ensuring faster load times.

In addition to keeping the file size to a manageable level, it's also advisable to limit your headline to the minimum number of words. Just give viewers enough to make them want to click on your banner and travel to your page. Then, leave it up to your web page headline and body copy to further involve and interest true prospects.

Banner headlines can appear in both a stationary and revolving format where only a portion of the total message is displayed at any given time. Both styles can work well to capture attention and generate interest.

"$203,281 Last Year With FREE ADVERTISING! Free 24-Page Report Reveals Inside Secrets. Get Rich Now..." (Jeff Gardner-- www.wealthworldplus.com)

"Click Here For A Fast, Affordable, Proven Tool To Help You Double Your Business -- Starting Tomorrow!"

"Safe, Natural Way To Remove Harmful Chemicals From All Fruits & Vegetables – 100% Guaranteed! Click Here"

"How To Boost Your Online Sales Effortlessly And Automatically!"

"Question: What's The #1 Key To Online Success? Answer: Make It Easy For More People To Buy From You Instantly! Here's How To Master The Secrets To Online Business In Just One Evening"

Signature Files

The best signature files serve irresistible messages designed to encourage viewers to click on the active link, whisking them off to your selected web page or blog. Essentially, it's a *headline* designed to get prospects to click to receive additional information from your visit your site, or via email.

Strong, compelling offers -- offers of free articles, reports, tips, audios, videos, and any other information of high-perceived value is what gets noticed. The higher the accepted value of the information offered and the more alluring it appears, the stronger the pull of the sig file. It also helps if the name attached has instant recognition amongst the audience. Recognized experts and authorities tend to attract more clicks because they've been "presold" to the audience to some degree.

Stimulate your readers interest. Arouse a little curiosity. Dangle a carrot that's difficult to ignore. Promise something that you know viewers would be interested in getting for themselves.

Sample signature files:

If you'd like to learn how a German businessman built a million dollar company with no advertising expense after reading my book, visit: www.frugalfun.com (Shel Horowitz)

Allan Gardyne
AssociatePrograms.com
Over 1,200 revenue sharing programs . . . and here's
the best one: email: best@AssociatePrograms.com

Gerry Robert is a best-selling author and operates the wildly successful Sales Mall web site. He offers FREE Moneymaking reports to anyone who drops by http://www.salesmall.com. If you have questions about Internet Marketing Success, his email address is: gerry@salesmall.com.

Jacques Werth
High Probability Selling
Acclaimed by the New York Times
and Entrepreneur magazine
http://www.highprobsell.com

Michel Fortin is a direct response copywriter, author, speaker, and consultant. Visit his blog and signup free to get blog updates by email, along with response-boosting tips, tested conversion strategies, the latest news, free advice, additional resources, and a lot more! Go now to http://www.michelfortin.com While you're at it, follow him on Twitter.

Judith
Enrich Your Soul,
Delight Your Eyes
And Improve Your Mind
Free Art Lesson And Free Booklets
http:// www.trabar.com

Email Messages

Most people scan their in-boxes and delete all messages that are either "spam" or those they're simply not interested in. For your emails to survive this initial screening process, you need to first of all make sure that your message complies with proper principles of "netiquette". This means that either:

1) someone has requested specific information from you... or...
2) they willingly subscribed to your mailing list... or...
3) they willingly added their name and address to a list in order to hear about various new products and offers.

Place your mini headline in the subject window. Ideally, you want to have interesting, attention-grabbing words upfront, so your message shows right away without the need to scroll sideways to make sense of your headline. Due to widespread spam and the subsequent need for email filters, finding effective words to use in your emails has become increasingly difficult.

Refine your headline down to a few short words that will kindle interest or arouse curiosity, causing recipients to want to open your mail. You can always follow up with the rest of your headline or subhead in the body of your message.

Here's a breakthrough idea from Gary Halbert that can get your email opened every time. It's most effective when you know the recipients full name and you can only use this technique sparingly, or it will quickly lose its effect.

"Are you the _____ _____ <insert actual first and last name> who _____ <insert identifying detail>

Example – *"Are you the Robert Boduch who wrote that book on headlines?"*

Like most people, I receive far more email than I can handle. It takes time to scan through my in-box, though I do my best to keep any time spent here to a minimum. But even though I didn't recognize the recipients name (a key ingredient when mailing to your list) I couldn't resist opening the email with the above headline.

Your subject header or headline plays a crucial role. You could have the finest, most-persuasive email sales copy ever written. But it's completely useless if your message doesn't get opened.

Curiosity-based headlines can also be effective when the senders name is recognized by the recipient. Below are a few examples used by marketers to their mailing lists:

"Secret Place Where Women Outnumber The Men 10 To 1" (Wayne Ross)

"I was nearly in tears..." (Joe Vitale)

"NLP Technique Adds $235,000 To Monthly Income " (Harlan Kilstein)

"Three Magic Words..." (Steve Manning)

"Could Your iphone Be The Most Dangerous Cell Phone Ever?" (Dr. Joseph Mercola)

"Weird test results" (Frank Kern)

"Gratis - My *13 point* secret checklist..." (Jo Han Mok)

Here are 5 tips to help to making an impact with your emails:

1. **Keep it short.** Email in-boxes are scanned at hyper-speed. That's why you've got to generate interest in just a few words. Get them to want to know more.

2. **Write to a single reader.** Even if you're mailing to thousands at once, you're still talking to one person at a time. One on one communication is key.

3. **Communicate value.** Make it more valuable to investigate/read further than to pass it up.

4. **Hit a hot button.** You need to know your readers and what will make an instant, gut-level impact. Recipients need to know that you understand their plight.

5. **Speak – don't shout.** Upper case text is the online equivalent of shouting. Strive to make an emotional connection by effectively leading readers with something interesting to them.

Forum/Discussion Board Postings

It's easy to see the types of headings that work well as discussion board leads. Check out any forum that displays the number of views each message attracts. Look long enough and you'll make a discovery. The postings that get the most attention fall into two categories:

1. They're either posted by a known author, such as the host of the board or, a recognized regular visitor or...

2. They feature a *provocative* or *riveting headline*.

Watch any forum or discussion board for a while and you'll quickly see the kind of headlines that draw the most traffic. These are the headlines that offer the something. They give value, promise a quick, easy, or free solution that fits nicely with the wants of the majority of board participants. The subject titles of these posts usually employ effective headline techniques.

Curiosity also has a strong pull on discussion boards, primarily due to the fast pace of "point & click" nature of the online world. Once curiosity is aroused, it interrupts the mental focus of the visitor, gently nudging in a direction that suggests satisfaction.

Appendix A:

Interviews With The Experts

Monique Harris is the author of *"How to Successfully Sell Information Products Online"* (www.SellYourBrainFood.com) as well as *"The Web Site Hosting and Designers Promotional Guide"*.

1) How important are headlines in your view, to the overall success of written communications?

Can you imagine a typical 7-page sales letter with no headlines? What about a 6-paneled brochure? Talk about one big run on sentence! You'd never get anybody to respond to your marketing message.

Good headlines are like lampposts on a dark road. Done effectively, they help guide the reader from Point A to Point B, in a smooth and efficient manner. When done ineffectively, they cause the reader to get lost, and quite often give up the task of reading your materials.

That's why you'll hear so many top copywriters say they take several hours - (or days) - to create dozens of headlines, before choosing the perfect one. They understand how that a well-timed headline, can make or break the sale, in a matter of seconds.

2) As an online marketing expert, what role would you say headlines play with respect to web pages, signature files, link titles, discussion board postings, ezine articles, etc. -- in their ability to "hook" interested prospects?

Most people underestimate the power of strategic headline usage on the Internet. For instance, if you were to visit my *SellYourBrainFood* site, which one of these headlines would you most be inclined to click on...

"Books For Sale" VERSUS "Learn How I'll Make My Fortune On the Internet"

They both advertise my manuals, but "Learn How I'll Make My Fortune On the Internet" is clearly the catchier of the two. (At least according to my web site visitors it is.) Plus, the second headline doesn't look as 'salesy' as the first.

One time when I was responding to a message in a Web forum, I decided to change the headline of the thread. It clearly made a difference, as my message was read twice as many times as the others. (There was a script installed which showed how many times each message had been read.)

And often when I'm skimming through email messages, the ones with the captivating subject lines get my attention first. The others typically get deleted. I imagine a lot of Netizens use this particular 'sorting' technique. Just one more reason for attractive headlines.

In the online world you've only got seconds to capture the audiences attention, as it's nothing for a prospect to simply click, and go elsewhere. So a well designed headline is very important when creating your Web pages, ezine articles, signature files, and so on.

3) How important are headlines to the results achieved with press releases? How do press release headlines differ from other marketing approaches?

Consider the fact that reporters and journalists receive dozens of press releases every single day. Oftentimes they'll just skim the headline of a release, and won't look at the actual copy, unless the headline itself is compelling.

In other words, if your release has a headline like, "New Book For Teachers," or "New Web Site Launched For Entrepreneurs," it's highly unlikely that it will receive much attention. These aren't 'headlines', they're 'DEADlines!'

Press release headlines must be constructed with the same care and skill, as any other headline, for any other marketing piece that you put together.

4) In your manual, you use sub-headings like, "The $85,000 Experiment That Taught Me A Very Valuable Lesson"... and.. "3 Magical Modules That Will Increase Your Info-products Value And

Sales Instantly." These headlines literally compel the reader to continue reading. Do you write such headlines beforehand, as part of an outline... or, do you create these gems as you write the copy?

I've tried doing the headline first, then writing the actual sections, but I find that this tends to limit me too much.

So what I do is create an outline of what I want to feature in each chapter. I then write the copy for each individual section. And lastly I do the headline, based on what's in each section.

It's easier to come up with a catchy headline once you have all the copy in place. In this way, you have something to actually base the headline on.

5) Do you have a favorite technique for writing headlines, or any simple tips you could share with readers of this manual?

I use numbers within my headlines, because people tend to like it when you break things down in steps. I also incorporate a lot of alliteration - (lumping words together with similar sounding beginnings) - because it makes the headline sound more catchy.

Here are a few examples which incorporate the two concepts:

"7 Steps for Creating a Profit Pulling Web Site"

"11 Easy Ways to Elevate Your E-zines Subscriber Base - Without Breaking a Sweat"

"10 Timely Marketing Ideas That'll Boost Your Business During the Holiday Season"

One final thing that I'd like to mention is that it's important to brainstorm on several different headlines before settling on one. There have been a few times when I've come up with two or three headlines, settled on one, and later realize that I could have done something a thousand times better, IF I had just taken a little extra time.

Do these little things, and you'll be surprised at the big results.

Ken Silver is the author of "How To Make $100,000 A Year In Your Spare Time Creating Profitable How-To Manuals" (www.ksilver.com)

1) How important are headlines in your view, to the overall success of written communications?

"Discover 5 little-known secrets that let you make a fortune on the Internet in less than a day!"

Did this sentence get your attention? If so, you've discovered how a headline is the ultimate attention-getter. A good headline makes you curious, often by promising to reveal further information by reading on. There are many ways you can do this... but the most important is by placing trigger words in this sentence, such as "discover," "little-known," "secrets" and "fortune." These simple words, when used in certain combinations, are a powerful formula.

Not only do they attract attention and inspire you to read further, but they should also promise to reveal - in a tantalizing way - what might be coming next.

There is nothing more powerful than a good headline. It is a true sales tool... one that opens the doors to allow the sales process to begin.

2) What advice would you give beginners regarding creating effective headlines?

There are many rules for writing effective and arresting headlines, but the most important are:

1. Put "you" in the headline wherever you can, to make the sentence user-friendly.

2. Where you can, personalize the headline statement. For example, in the headline above we could say: *"Self-taught millionaire farmer tells you how to discover 5 little-known secrets that let you make a fortune on the Internet in less than a day!"* Putting a real person into the headline makes it believable. I have tested my own headlines and seen

248

up to a 50% improvement when I placed terms in them like: "50 year-old publisher..."

3. Get money into the headline. Whether you use the term "millionaire," or a fixed amount as I do - "$100,000 a year..." - income is a vital feature of every successful headline. Don't write yours without a mention of at least one financial promise.

4. Inject some personality into your copy! This is because - as we are all rapidly coming to understand in e-land - there is an excess of me-too products out there, all striving mightily for recognition. It's causing a regular product and information traffic jam that's getting worse by the day. So people turn off of the generic promises. They crave direct communication with real people. Warm bodies. Smiling, people with a genuine concern for their well-being.

Can you put that in your headlines? Can you bring a real live, breathing human being into your headline copy? My suggestions:

* Use a name. For example, one of my daughters was Miss Wellington (my home city) a few years back. So: *"19 Year-old Miss Wellington Shares Her Winning Beauty Secrets"* would be a starting point here.

* Give your headline some action. Not passive, stodgy nouns, but movement, involvement. Ask your reader to DO something now... not just flick the page. Use words like "Now," "Get" and "Use" to motivate.

* Get in touch with your reader's pressing need for human involvement.

3) How would you rate (in terms of a percentage) the relative importance of headlines, to the success of the following individual applications:

Sales letter:
90%. Your letter shouldn't simply start off "Dear Sir," or even "Dear Friend." Instead, put a proactive headline at the top of your letter and watch sales soar!

Brochure:
50%. Many brochures are simply reference material, and the least powerful and effective part of a sales strategy. In fact, it has been

proven that some mail-order packages pull fewer responses when a brochure is included. One of the many disadvantages of a brochure, apart from the cost, is that when something in your organization changes, i.e.; phone numbers, addresses and prices, it makes your glossy brochure immediately obsolete. I wouldn't recommend using a brochure.

Book/ Manual:

75%. Although I would still give as much attention to the title of the book or manual as any other part of the sales package, it is less important when you have a sales letter do the main selling job for you. Even so, you can't disregard the impact of a good book or manual title on your sales.

Newspaper Display Ad:

100%. There is no doubt that the headline is the most crucial part of any advertisement. It serves as a banner to draw the reader in, and should be given the highest priority in your sales message. To be most effective, a newspaper headline should have a deadline within it. In fact, where possible, you should place a deadline or time frame in all your headlines. Look again at the headline at the top of this article. Notice that it gives a promise in time. It is a powerful incentive for reader action.

Press Release

75%. A strong selling headline is not important here... all you are trying to do use catch the editor's attention, and often a statement is a better course of action. The editors will write their own headline on your article, so don't waste time trying to predict what they will do.

Web Page:

90%. If you are following an effective marketing strategy, and using your e-zine as a link for prospects, then the headline on your Web Page need not be 100% effective.

Signature File:

50%. Your signature file is important of course, and here you have to work hard to get as much information as you can into a small space. My own one is quite wordy:

Ken Silver

The "How-To" Guru!
^^^

Digital Book Author
"How To Make $100,000 A Year Part-Time Creating
How-To Manuals At Home"
Read the first chapter and contents FREE!
Visit: http://www.ksilver.com

Member of the Self Publishing
Association of New Zealand

Join me on the Ken Silver Online Forum:
www.netbabbler.com/goto?forumid=11488
^^^

4) Do you prefer longer or shorter headlines? Why?

A long headline every time! You might attract attention from a few
readers by putting something has small as a question mark at the top
of your document, but there is no doubt that the more information you
can give - the better response you will get.

**5) How many potential headlines do you typically generate for every
headline that is actually tested in the marketplace?**

The more headlines I write the sooner I find the ideal one. I often
write 20 or 30 headline changes before settling on the perfect
combination of words and promises. It is quite usual for the final cut
to be very similar to the first few headlines I attempt. Some
copywriters don't feel they have discovered the best headline until
they have written several hundred combinations. Most of us don't have
the luxury of time or persistence to do this... and the slight
improvement in response may not be critical enough for us to be
concerned with.

The real answer is to balance up the amount of time you have against
what you have to complete. Write as many headlines as you need to do
the job.

Wanda Loskot is a Business Coach and Marketing Expert (www.loska.com)

1) How important are headlines in your view, to the overall success of written communications?

Extremely important. Some experts say that 90% of the effectiveness depends on the headline - that means that for every dollar you spend, 90 cents is invested in the headline. Funny thing is that usually people spend much more time creating and editing the body of an ad, letter, article, etc. - and the headline or title is just created on the spur of the moment. BIG mistake. If the reader does not find the title interesting, intriguing or at least... annoying or controversial - he will not read the rest, most of the time.

2) What are some common mistakes small business owners make regarding headlines?

In advertising, the biggest one is using their own name - or bragging about their business. Ads like "ATB Enterprises - established in 1992" make me laugh, although they are really sad. This one is a real example from my newsletter. It is a fencing company - a simple headline "Fences" would work much better.

Another mistake is writing those cute headlines that are unusual and make people think before they can figure out what is this all about. One of the dumbest ones I've ever seen was "Go to the Head of the Class" in an ad for the apartment leasing office!

People don't like to be challenged in print advertising - they have enough challenges in their lives. The easier the reading, the smoother it is and the easier to understand - the more likely they will read the rest.

3) How do you know when you've got a dynamite headline?

Aaaaaah, this is a dynamite question!

I think it would be the headline that your (and only your) target reader sees and it is so grabbing that they feel they just have to read it now.

Those great headlines are usually bold, startling sentences.
Awesome offers, big time news, provocative statements...

My favorite headline of all times *is* *"Let's Give The Blacks What
They Deserve"* - it was created in the time when parts of Washington DC
were still in ruins after the riots in connection with the assassination
of Dr. Martin Luther King Jr. and it was an advertisement for a bank
lending money to the black community! Needless to say - the ad created
not only readership and response, but also quite a stir and... additional
publicity for that lending institution and for the ad creator, Stan Cotton.

Stan is a brilliant advertising man who is often called the modern day
Claude Hopkins (who is the biggest legend in advertising). I highly
recommend Stan Cotton's book "Anybody Can Be in Advertising... It
Beats Working for a Living!" (here is another great title!) - his site is
http://quitjob.com

**4) What is it about one headline that makes it a huge success, while
another headline fails miserably?**

I don't think that it would be safe for me to answer this in such
a generic way. Headlines should be tested because without testing, even
the greatest advertising guru will make mistakes, so it is difficult
to say which ad will do extremely well and which will not likely do so,
so...

When the headline is "me-centered" it is the kiss of death.
Headline should always say "Hey you, you are the person I want
to talk to - here is something you must read now".

I have on my site the entire book by Claude Hopkins (Scientific
Advertising) free for all to read online. There is a terrific chapter about
headlines: http://www.loska.com/hopkins/5.html - extremely helpful for
anyone who is thinking about writing any marketing communication.

**5) Do you have any examples of great headlines that you can share
with our readers?**

As a matter of fact, I do! I have a piece called "The Best 100 Headlines Ever Written" - http://www.loska.com/columns/headlines.html

6) What 3 tips would you suggest to help our readers write more effective headlines?

1). Take time! Remember that the headline is the key to the rest of the piece. You should spend MOST of the time on creating a powerful, attention-grabbing headline, and the rest of the time on the body of the ad. Not vice versa.

2). Make it startling, bold, provocative, newsworthy. If you put an offer in the headline - make it BIG.

3). Concentrate on your target reader and speak to him/her. If you can name him - do so. Headline like *"Attention residents of the Whispering Hills in Carrboro"* make it impossible for residents of Whispering Hills not to read it!

Appendix B:

Checklist For Effective Headline Writing

- ❏ Is this headline loaded with attention-getting words designed to stop readers in their tracks and draw their interest?

- ❏ Is a specific audience identified and targeted?

- ❏ Does the headline deliver a captivating and complete statement that makes readers want to read on?

- ❏ Is it specific?

- ❏ Does it woo the reader into the body copy?

- ❏ Is it as powerful as it can be?

- ❏ Does it intrigue?

- ❏ Does it offer a solution?

- ❏ Does it remind prospects of their anxiety?

- ❏ Does it make a huge promise?

- ❏ Does it appeal to the prospect's self-interest?

- ❏ Does it supply news?

- ❏ Is it very clear at first reading or is it confusing with 2 or more possible meanings?

- ❏ Could curiosity be added to increase the appeal?

- ❏ Does it say what you want it to say?

- ❏ Does it offer the most valuable benefit?

- ❏ Is it believable?

❑ Is the message of the headline focused on my intended audience?

❑ Would the message be enhanced with the use of a photograph?

❑ Could the headline be made more visually captivating with any additional graphic enhancements?

❑ Does it call out to your target audience with a message that's of specific importance to them?

Appendix C:

Suggested Reading

The Robert Collier Letter Book by Robert Collier

Direct Mail Copy That Sells! by Herschel Gordon Lewis

The Ultimate Sales Letter by Dan Kennedy

The Copywriters Handbook by Robert W. Bly

How To Write A Good Advertisement by Victor Schwab

Tested Advertising Methods by John Caples

How To Make Your Advertising Make Money by John Caples

Cash Copy by Jeffrey Lant

Ogilvy On Advertising by David Ogilvy

Magic Words That Bring You Riches by Ted Nicholas

The Copy Workshop by Bruce Bendinger

Maxwell Sackheim's Billion Dollar Marketing by Jerry Buchanan/ David Reecher

Creating Successful Small Business Advertising by Jerry Fisher

The Greatest Direct Mail Sales Letters Of All Time by Richard S. Hodgson

Million Dollar Mailings by Denison Hatch

How To Make Maximum Money In Minimum Time! by Gary Halbert

Advertising Magic by Brian Keith Voiles

Scientific Advertising by Claude Hopkins

Words That Sell by Richard Bayan

Phrases That Sell by Edward Werz and Sally Germain

Influence... The Psychology Of Persuasion by Dr. Robert Cialdini

The AMA Complete Guide To Small Business Advertising by Joe Vitale

CyberWriting: How to Promote Your Product or Service Online (without being flamed) by Joe Vitale

The Power of Outrageous Marketing! Using the 10 time-tested

secrets of titans, tycoons, and billionaires to get rich in your own business by Joe Vitale (audio program)
Unlimited Power by Anthony Robbins

Made in the USA
Lexington, KY
14 November 2015